"Be forewarned. This book, like Danaan's workshops and projects, is wise and effective. It might just change your life."

ROBERT GILMAN: Founder and Editor of *In Context* journal

PeaceTrees

*For every tree that is used up to print these books,
Sunstone/Earthstewards Network plants two trees,
through the international PeaceTrees program of the Earthstewards Network.*

WARRIORS
OF THE
HEART

DANAAN PARRY

Sunstone Publications

WARRIORS
of the
HEART

1st Printing: January 1991
2nd Printing: July 1991
3rd Printing: March 1993
4th Printing: October 1994

ISBN: 0-913319-09-0
Library of Congress Catalog Number: 90-070815

Illustrations by Marksman Studio
Typesetting and Graphics by Ms. Prints
Cover Design by Doreen DeNicola

printed on recycled paper

Published by
Sunstone Publications
RD 4 Box 700AW
Cooperstown, NY 13326
U.S.A.

(607) 547-8207

ACKNOWLEDGEMENTS

Many thanks to —

- Happi McQuirk, who not only can type and edit, but also, unlike me, can spell.

- Roger Day, who can miraculously make computers talk to each other.

- All the people in the Earthstewards Network

- The hundreds of folks who have been crazy enough to come with me into unknown, scary places on the planet and inside ourselves.

- Agnes Marie Murray Parry, who told me I could do it.

- Lori, my publisher and editor and sister Warrior.

TABLE OF CONTENTS

FORWARD

To Trust . . .

Most meet Danaan first as a teacher. I met him first as a tourist. We were in Leningrad together. My first experience of the Hermitage and St. Isaacs was with him. The contrast was striking — the rich simplicity of Danaan and the ornate complexity of the cathedral and the museum. And yet, the astounding beauty of the lapis lazuli and malachite, the thousands of man hours of sanding and polishing they represented, struck a chord with Danaan. His polishing has been internal. The splendour shines in the cathedral of his mind and spirit; he has mastered the art of keeping the lines of communication between every antenna of his being completely pure.

I realized I had found a man I could trust.

Our paths don't cross much. I tend to be nervous and hyperactive, rushing around the world, organizing external things, afraid of trying to organize me. I lack the relaxed consciousness that Danaan exudes. Yet our field is the same: citizen diplomacy, harmony between people, earth stewardship and empowering young people to take responsibility for stewardship. A lot of weird stuff happens in our field that makes it hard to live at peace with oneself or others. Conflict bristles, there are jealousies, and often a crushing sense of failure or impotence. I deal with it badly.

Knowing Danaan has helped me. His strong calm demonstrates that all is somehow meant to be. We have to pass through the agony to get to any kind of Peace. As Danaan says, "the eye of the hurricane is the only safe place to be." I did his workshop in May; I felt my mind and spirit needed time in the shop after forty years. My trust in him was deepened. Also, my trust in myself. It was extraordinary to be in a room full of people with the most appalling problems - divorce, family troubles, personal crises that started at birth and seem to have continued ever since. And yet at the end of the workshop they all stood up and, with quivering intensity, affirmed: "I am a great person. I am incredibly powerful!"

When I stood up, I talked about my doubts about my own power. Typical British modesty — rather an attractive quality, I used to feel. Wrong! Danaan asked us to write ourselves a letter. I wrote, "My power is enraged by me! How dare I doubt the power! I have to stop feeling inadequate. Let your power really express itself. I love you so much. Remember that . . . "

I got the letter last week just as I was about to undertake a huge Peace Concert at the United Nations. I was terrified. The letter, out of the blue, totally reaffirmed my faith in myself. That's what this book will do for you. It will lead you back to that powerful part of yourself where your doubts and modesty disappear — where you can be your true, powerful Cathedral Self. Trust him.

In every line of this book, there is a sense of his searching integrity. And yet in accepting trust, you accept betrayal — the Peter kind of betrayal, betrayal through fear or inadequacy, which ends up in strengthening trust. Not the Judas betrayal which ends in suicide. In this book there may be things that don't work for you. That should not break your trust. We all screw up — we all misinterpret. Even Danaan. That should strengthen our commitment. For in Danaan's perfect metaphor of the trapeze, we cast off from the first trapeze in the certain faith that we shall catch the one that is flying towards us. But what if we don't?? It's a fair question. Danaan's answer is that we shall experience the even more stupendous reality of learning to fly. Believe it!

David Woollcombe

David is the founder and Executive Director of the Peace Child Foundation which has brought together youths from the USA, Soviet Union, Great Britain, Costa Rica, Nicaragua, and other nations in hundreds of performances of the play "Peace Child" all over the world.

INTRODUCTION

WARRIORS OF THE HEART

This book is for every woman and man who is ready to accept responsibility for their part in the passionate, positive change process that is about to transform our planet.

As I Have The Power
So Must I Have The Courage
Shine It On The Earth

Russ

This is a book about you — the possible you, the one who has that somehow unexplainable feeling that you were meant for something more, that your life has a greater purpose.

This is a field manual for all those who know (maybe not understand, but know) that they have somehow chosen to be a part of something very new, something that could bring our species from the brink of destruction to the doorway of an entirely new concept of human relationships.

Our planet is crying out for men and women to own their power and to be positive agents of peaceful change. This book is about you learning to do just that.

The Warrior of the Heart is someone who is making a difference, a positive difference with their life. It may happen in a remote village or on international television. Perhaps no one knows about it but you and your children, or you and the city council, or perhaps thousands are involved — that doesn't matter.

What does matter is that, because the Warrior of the Heart has had the courage and commitment to live what she or he believes, the world is a better place to live and the conscious evolution of our species has moved forward one more notch.

That potential for conscious, positive change is present and alive in every one of us. For most, it lies sleeping beneath the years of conditioning to "mind your own business," "don't rock the boat," and "you can't change anything." Those condition-ings are lies which we use to stay asleep or to stay "safe." But the state of our planet tells us that it is no longer safe to sleepwalk through life.

Moving Through Fear
To Live In Shadow And Light
To Love With Passion

Diane

As you read through this book, you will encounter a variety of personal stories and quotes relating to the elements of Heart Warriorship. They serve to change the flow from the traditional page after page of ideas and concepts to a tapestry of related but different ways of looking at and living your path as Warrior of the Heart. Hopefully, this will stimulate and challenge you to make these concepts relevant to your own life.

You will also notice the short three line verse at the beginning of some sections. This is Haiku. Haiku is a Japanese tone poem wherein the structure of 5-7-5 guides you to express your feelings simply and clearly in the moment. The first line has five syllables, the second line has seven and the third line has five. Try it for yourself.

The Haiku in this book were written during Warrior of the Heart Advanced Trainings in Virginia and Washington. They tell of the pain and the joy one encounters as one embraces the Warrior path in a new way.

1

PREPARING TO BE THE NEW WARRIOR

"The Warrior's Job is to bring change to the Tribe"
- Yaqui teaching

1
The Warrior Path - Ancient and New

2
Leadership as a Warrior Path

3
What About Heroes?

4
New Definitions for a New Way of Thinking

Chapter 1

The Warrior Path - Ancient and New

Facing The Question
Searching, Finding, Committing
I Am Peacemaker
Warren

Our world needs women and men who are willing to walk the Warrior path today, who will bring Warrior-energy into their daily lives and live each day with the commitment, the aliveness and the awareness of the Warrior.

**"NOTHING
IS AS IMPORTANT
AS THIS DAY"**
-Goethe

Do you need to totally change your life to follow the Warrior way? Must you go to some mountaintop temple to train for twenty years? Of course not. In fact, since we live in the twentieth century and not the fourteenth, you would probably be running away from the unlocking of your own inner Warrior rather than the embracing of it. Given the state of our planet, you and I are called upon to "learn on the job." We are here to become aware of the Warrior spirit right where we are in the midst of the day-to-day life we have created for ourselves, rather than to run off anywhere else trying to find it.

We are fortunate that many of the techniques and awarenesses that have been part of the inner training of the Warrior down through the centuries are still known in bits and pieces through the wisdom teachings of many traditions. My work over the years has been to bring together these bits and pieces and to present them in ways that make the training of the peaceful Warrior available to our present culture right where we are. You and I need to breathe life into our own peaceful Warriors right here in the middle of our love relationships, on our jobs, in the marketplace and in our social and political selves; exactly what this book is meant to do.

How to Use This Book

To begin to evoke your own inner Warrior, read through this book. Then, when you are ready to seriously begin the process of Warriorship, go through the book again, this time doing each exercise in turn. Create the space in your life for the activities mentioned. You should take no more than six months to complete all initial activities and exercises. To drag out the process longer than six months dilutes the impact of the process on your psyche.

Obviously, this path requires you to be serious about your growth and to embrace the idea of *commitment* in your life. Please do not think that you can simply read through the book, do a few random exercises and still be unlocking your inner Warrior. You can't. This doesn't mean that reading the book alone is useless. Whatever you can and are willing to do with this information will trigger some new/ancient awarenesses in you. Do what you can, but please don't go around calling yourself a "Warrior of the Heart" unless you have completed the full training. Integrity is one of the most important attributes of the heart-centered Warrior.

There is a legend centered in the time when the Chinese overran Tibet. On a mountain in the Himalayas, there was a Tibetan Buddhist monastery. A village had grown at its gate. When the people in the village learned that the Chinese Army was advancing, everyone fled. Upon arrival at the village, the commander of the Chinese battalion was furious that there were no crowds that could be forced into submissive cheers of welcome. He ordered that his soldiers go up to the monastery and disembowel all the monks. Soon his lieutenant came down with the news that all the monks had fled except one, the abbot of the monastery, and that he had a strange energy about him that frightened the soldiers and they would not go near him. Out-

raged, the commander whipped his horse up the trail, through the gates and found the abbot in meditation. The commander dismounted, swaggered over to the abbot and drew his sword. He rested the tip of his sword on the rope belt of the abbot's cloak and sneered, "Don't you know who I am? Don't you know that with one push on this sword I could skewer your belly?"

The abbot raised his eyes from meditation, smiled curiously and said, "Yes, I know who you are. Don't you know who I am? Don't you know that with one push on this sword I could have you skewer my belly?"

It is said that the confused commander sheathed his sword and rode away.

Within this simple story lies all the elements of the Warrior way. Of course, the abbot was the true Warrior, the heart Warrior, not the pompous soldier.

In every ancient tradition that embraces the concept of the peaceful Warrior, several elements continuously appear:

> Commitment
> Integrity
> Inner Calm
> Sense of Self
> Intensity
> Focused Power (Will)
> Compassion
> Awareness of a greater reality
> Use of ritual and symbol
> Responsibility to the Whole
> A joy-filled sense of wonder about new-ness
> Inner courage
> Humility

> **"The hottest places in hell are reserved for those who, in times of great moral crisis, maintain their neutrality."**
> *Dante*

The world is drowning in its own mediocrity. Excitement and aliveness have often been relegated to the hollow characters on television soap operas. Yet deep within us, we feel the call of the spirit urging us to fully embrace the life we have been given. The path of the Warrior of the Heart is to live life fully, consciously and passionately. In a fascinating and synchronistic way, when you choose this Warrior path, you at once free your own inner spirit and you also participate in the move towards that same freedom for others. The path of the Warrior of the Heart requires you to be conscious, attuned to your part in the greater drama of life on earth.

The word "Warrior" bothers many people. It has been associated with misuse of power, with dominance over others. However, the concept of the Warrior was not originally connected to war and aggression, and it is time that we reclaimed the true meaning of this ancient and powerful concept. The Buddhist tradition defines the Warrior as "one who has the courage to know oneself." Now why do you suppose that the Buddhists felt that one would require courage in order to know oneself? Because they were talking about knowing *all* of oneself, not just the nice parts, the bright side, but the darkness in oneself as well. They knew that the only real battles you as a Warrior must face are the inner ones, where you go inside and face your inner dragons. The secret is that the Warrior does not slay the dragons; the Warrior transforms their energy into positive power and gives it back to the world in this transformed state.

In keeping with this connection between the Warrior path and inner courage, the even more ancient Tibetan definition of a "warrior" is "one who faces one's own fear." Note that neither definition has anything to do with one's outside reality, they both define the Warrior path as inside your own being.

The Yaqui Indians, the indigenous peoples of the mountains in northern Mexico, define the concept of the Warrior in a wonderful way. They say that in each tribe certain men and women are called to follow the Warrior way. They are called from inside their own heart. From an external viewpoint, it would be difficult to identify these people because an important part of the Warrior way is to look upon oneself with humility, as "nobody special." The Warrior simply has a very specific role to play within the tribe. They are the ones who bring newness into the world.

The Yaqui say that our "conceptual reality," that which everybody agrees is real, is like the tabletop of our kitchen table. All of your, mine and everyone's experience of "reality" is piled on the tabletop (the Yaqui call it the tonal). We all agree that nothing else is real; it's all on this tabletop. But true reality, the larger reality, is the tabletop and everything else in all directions to infinity (the Nagual). It is the Warrior's role to bring back what she or he discovers and to add it to the tabletop so that everyone's conceptual reality expands. The tabletop gets bigger for everyone.

The Yaqui say that our everyday world is something like a play, a performance. I describe it as a movie. We're all watching the movie. We're all playing in the movie, too. Just like in a movie theatre, as we watch, the movie goes from reel one to reel two to reel three, four, etc. Because the projectionist is a professional, we never notice the changes from reel to reel. It appears as one continuous show. But the Warrior notices!

In this movie metaphor, the role of the Warrior is to stay awake, *really* awake, so that when the projectionist (I'm talking about *The* Projectionist with a capital P) changes reels, the Warrior sees that change. The Warrior looks out between the reels and becomes aware of the reality behind the movie. The Warrior, for an instant, sees the Play behind the play. The Warrior brings that truth back to us all and shares it, and thus our conceptual reality grows and deepens.

The Yaqui say that *this growth of conceptual reality* is the only way that true change happens. When a Warrior has the commitment to stay awake, when a Warrior has the courage to see beyond the movie and then bring that vision back and share it, true change occurs. The Yaqui say this is the only real change process. All else is pseudo-change.

Chapter 2

Leadership as a Warrior Path

Opening Myself
Telling The Truth About Me
My Path To God
Lin

The effective management of change is a vital part of being the new Warrior of the Heart. It calls for a new model of facilitative servant-leadership, one that empowers rather than controls.

It's hard for me to believe that my very first taste of this new kind of leadership didn't occur until my early thirties. Prior to that, every model of leadership had been the old win/lose, hard model of power. And then there was Abe....

I had been a scientist with the Atomic Energy Commission at their laboratory in Livermore, California for about six years. I had just been promoted to project manager, which thrust me out of the laboratory and into a management position without any training in how to manage people. Terrified, I looked around for some training that would teach me how to deal with human beings as well as I had been taught to deal with electrons, cloud chambers and quantum levels. I found a few short courses in traditional management theory and that helped me to cope with time-lines and budgets, but no one was talking about people, about how to deal with their feelings and wants and fears. As I look back, I see that I was really searching for some way to deal with my own internal desires and fears and confusion.

I began to notice that, in my inadequacy as a manager, I had adopted a "get-tough" style of leadership, which was really a "don't let them see how frightened you are" style. My bosses loved me for it; my subordinates were beginning to hate me for it.

One morning, one of my engineers walked into my office, his face drawn and white, his tie hanging crooked and limp around his neck. He had obviously been awake all night. His name was Sam, a long drink of water from Tennessee with a drawl as long as he was. Now, the day before, I had told Sam to whip up a budget for his part of our project, because I needed it this morning to take to the director for approval. Sam leaned weakly on my desk and said that he had not been able to finish the budget. I could sense that something was very wrong with Sam and he looked on the brink of tears. I felt the terror build in my stomach and throat. If I wasn't very careful, this guy was going to let his feelings out, all over my office and, well, we couldn't have that, could we?

And then it came, my worst fear. His tears. Through them he blurted out his story. He had come home from work the night before to find a note from his wife on the kitchen table. She was gone, with the two kids, with every penny in their savings account, without a trace. He had been on the phone all night trying to find her, with no hope left in him.

And now he was looking at me, through wet, red eyes. Waiting for me to respond, to reach out to him in some way. I tell you true that I have since been in bombings, shoot-outs and riots where my life hung by a lucky thread, but I have never been as scared as when Sam looked at me, his soul ripped open and exposed to my reply. He was asking me to feel. Damn him, doesn't he know I don't know how! Men, even equals, don't expose themselves to each other like this. And I'm his boss! This will not do!

And so I said it. Out of the depths of unspoken fear and unacknowledged pain in me, I said that which has lived with me for fifteen years. I said, "Sam, we don't pay you to bring your domestic problems to the office." I think he died a little then. I know I did. He slithered out of my office. I fell back in my chair and from something still alive in me came the cry, "Oh, Danaan, you need help so bad." I thought my head would explode.

Proving that there are indeed no coincidences in the world, the very next day a colleague told me about an "organizational dynamics" course at U.C.L.A. for managers.

Desperately, I applied and was accepted. The "course" turned out to be an intense T-Group (Encounter Group) at Ojai, California where ten middle-management types from ten different companies were "locked-up" in a suite of rooms for seven days, with a leading psychologist or psychiatrist in attendance with each group of ten. If I had known that before arriving in Ojai, I would have never gone near the place. But there we were, ten slick, up and coming bright young men, groomed for the top and defensive as hell. And there was Abe, Professor Abe, Dean of Psychology at Haifa University, Israel, with a list of titles as long as his beard. The rules were that we could have all the food and drink we wanted but, except for an occasional all-group lecture, we could not leave the suite of rooms for seven days.

"Piece of cake," I said. I can coast through this untouched. I don't know what the unspoken rules are, but I'm an expert at finding them out, so no sweat.

The first day, we were so pleasant to each other. I gave my credentials, my impressive education and my accomplishments. We all did. Professor Abe said perhaps ten words the whole day. On the second day, we ten felt each other out some more, established a pecking order, discerned each other's weak points and nerve-endings. By the end of day two, we had run out of conversation, out of games, out of patience.

On the third morning, someone told the group how fed-up he was with the rest of us, how shallow he thought we were. We ate him alive. Like a team of piranha, we systematically tore him apart emotionally and picked his bones clean. When he was a pile of quivering rubble, we turned on the next-weakest member and did the same. Finally, here was a vent for our resentments and fears, and we used all the skill we had accumulated on our paths to becoming managers to viciously attack each other. By the fourth day, we had attacked everyone. I had been folded, spindled and mutilated, too, but somehow it felt familiar. Isn't that what men are supposed to do to each other? How else could they relate to one another under these circumstances?

Then we remembered Abe. And we attacked him. We were good at it, screaming incompetence, hurling charges of mediocrity and stupidity at him, firing thinly veiled arrows of anti-Semitism his way. After all, he had just sat there for four days, apart from an occasional comment or suggestion, which were of course all nonsense and useless to us. How dare he call himself a professional. We were surely going to advise our superiors to demand our tuition back and sue this charlatan for malpractice.

But it wasn't working. Our teeth weren't ripping his flesh. He wasn't biting our hooks, wasn't taking our bait. And yet he wasn't protecting himself, either. He wasn't defending his position. He was just there. It was like he could take in the whole world and love it and feel it and not be crumbled by it. Damn him!

I told him he was a fake and he asked me how I felt when I said that. I told him he didn't give a shit about me or how I felt, so stop pretending. He asked me if my father had ever given a shit about how I felt and I started to cry. Oh, God, not now, not in front of all these men, please — I'll do anything not to cry. Please.

And he's got his arms around me and he's holding me. And he's telling me about his father who died in a Nazi concentration camp and he's crying and I'm telling him about my father who never touched me, never told me he loved me and I'm crying. Sweet Jesus, we're just out there on the rug on our knees and our tears are smeared all over our faces and we're hugging. And there's a part of my brain that's still hanging on, still analyzing the situation and it's saying, "They're looking at you, you fool. They'll use this against you. You're hugging another man, you're crying and you cannot do this!" But that part of me is getting smaller and smaller and the rest of me is just there, with the tears, mine and Abe's, and our bodies tight together and it feels so, so good. Oh, God, if my father had pressed his body against mine like this. If he had cried with me, not just when he was stinking drunk. But this is now and I'm healing; I am feeling. I can feel and it's so, so good.

In the final three days, we somehow were able to reach past the years of deadness and confront and comfort and heal one another. Not everyone, but most of us, learned to cry and to touch and to feel, together. And Abe was just there. A word here, a story there, a hug, a laugh, a shared pain.

I had found that I could feel. I found something else that week in Ojai, although it would take me ten years to fully comprehend it. I had found a model of a new way of using power, of leadership. It is the force that can heal the world.
My first act when we were "let out" was to call Sam and ask for his forgiveness. It is again no coincidence that when my own marriage fell apart one year later, Sam was there by my side to comfort me.

As I write about my experience with Abe at Ojai, I realize that, after more than fifteen years, it is still primarily a feeling, emotional learning memory for me. I know this because I cried, deliciously, as I wrote about it just now. However, these many years later, it is also important to look at what Abe was doing in our group of managers that not only allowed me to feel my feelings and experience, a breakthrough which changed my life, but which also modelled a new form of leadership. He *lived* a way of using power in a group (that's a definition of leadership) that I had never experienced before; one that planted seeds in me which began to sprout ten years later when I entered the field of international conflict resolution. So, what was Abe doing with me? What was he *not* doing?

One of the things he did (or *somebody* did) was to *"create a safe space."* This jargon expresses what has become the first rule of conflict resolution, as I have formulated it in my work and teaching. It is impossible to resolve a conflict, or to bring a group of people to a deep level of sharing unless you have first created a psychological and physical "space" within which the work can be done.

Secondly, Abe *"allowed conflict."* Such a simple statement and so difficult, usually, to achieve. You and I have been taught from birth (or before) that conflict is not okay. It is dangerous and to be avoided at all costs. Furthermore, we are taught that if you avoid it, if you pretend there is no conflict when there really is, that it will all ultimately "go away." Just pretend long enough and it will disappear. That is, of course, a lie. Conflict (when it appears) will not "go away." Instead it will, when denied, go *underground.* It will burrow deep into your body and psyche. It's like pretending that a wound really isn't infected when it is and covering it with a tight bandage so you can't see it. It then spreads internally, infecting the entire organism, becoming much more difficult to heal.

Abe let us play our games. He let us run our numbers. He knew we would run out of patience and cover-ups and niceness, and then when the conflict surfaced, he "allowed" it. He let us rip the band-aids off each other's wounds, so that the air and sun could get at them. But he also, ever-so-subtly, directed the energy. I can see in hindsight that we never really did annihilate anyone. When we got close to it, when someone was close to their limit, he would comment on the unfairness of another, or the similarity of one of us to the poor victim and so we would leave the original focus of our vengeance and redirect it at the next victim. We all were shaken, but not toppled. We all were bent, but far from broken. We all were brought to a common experience of seeing our old defenses and games, which had worked for years, not working anymore. There's no reason to let go of old ways of being and explore newness if the old ways still work.

Abe was *present*. Just as most of us have been taught to avoid conflict, so too we have developed ways of manifesting our avoidance. We have learned to "disappear," either physically or perhaps just psychologically. When the going gets tough, when any amount of unpleasantness or disagreement surfaces, we "go out to lunch." This gives rise to the saying, "his lights are on but nobody's home," as we look into the blank eyes of someone who has taken their consciousness somewhere else so as to avoid the unpleasant moment.

Abe didn't do that. He stayed. He was totally present, available, to each moment, to each attack on him, to every game and avoidance technique we tried. He did not judge them or us. He was just there, open to us. He was, in some indefinable way, vulnerable and yet strong, soft and yet unbreakable. Like water. That's it, it was as if we were throwing rocks in the sea. He could take them all, not needing to throw any back at us. He remained the sea, powerful and available to us. Somehow that allowed us to do what we needed to do to cleanse ourselves. It gave us permission to be the nasty little rock-throwing adolescent boys that we were never allowed to be when we *were* adolescents, in a "safe space" where we could let go of our armloads of rocks and then see who we really were under that pile.

Abe was able to *let go of his position*. From the moment I met him as I tentatively peeked in the door of the suite of rooms at Ojai, it was quite obvious that this man was a professional. As I furiously re-read the brochure to establish who he was (which for me at that time meant *what* he was, how many degrees and from where), I had an insight that he was much more than any degree on that sheet of paper (which scared the pants off of me, because for me, people *were* what it said on that paper).

Yet, on that fourth day when we were kneeling on the floor, our bodies heaving and sobbing in rhythm, his cracking voice telling me about his father who never came back from the concentration camp, he was only Abe. There was no clever act there to induce us to "break." His guts were all over the rug, his vulnerability to me totally present, his pain unhidden.

Sure, at some moment prior to our body-to-body encounter, he probably held some mental picture of how he could assist me in my growth. But out there on the floor was no PhD. psychotherapist, no head of department at the University of Haifa. Out there was Abe, vulnerable, soft, available, with no labels in sight. He brought to that moment something that I have come to see as *the* most important element in leadership, in peacemaking, in just being a human being — *INTEGRITY.*

It takes integrity, courage, and a deep sense of self to be able to "let go of one's position." And these are qualities of the Warrior of the Heart. These are the characteristics of the new path of leadership, new politics, new relationship. When your use of your own power does not depend on your external *position*, but on a deep feeling of connection to your internal source, your SELF, then you can allow yourself to relinquish your *position*, your need to be *right* at all costs. Only then are you able to hear the other person. Only then can you create the environment within which real healing, real win-win outcomes can occur.

It's so easy to get stuck in our *positions*, because we are taught that, in some vague way, we *are* our positions and if we let go of them we'll lose. Lose what? It doesn't matter. The fear of losing is so great, the worry about appearing foolish, or stupid, or unlovable is so engrained and terrifying, that we feel we *must* defend our position or die.

What do I mean by "our position?" It usually has to do with "being right" or "this is the way *it* is" or "this is who *I* am, nothing else." You hear people say, "Well, that's just the way I am" or "Well, out in the *real* world...." Our position might be, "Look, I'm the trained teacher here...(or therapist, or M.D., or mommie, or the man in the family, or...)." We've got it all figured out, we know how it works and we don't want any more input.

I learned a lot from Abe in those few days. He gave me a model for a new way of using power, a new way to be a leader through empowerment and giving permission. That kind of leadership allows people to feel that *they* did it and can do it again. That kind of leadership doesn't create a few gurus; it creates thousands of empowered people who are ready to take responsibility for their own lives. That kind of leadership is a Warrior of the Heart.

In the field generically known as "peace-work," we're loaded with *positions*. "My definition of peace is better than their definition." "Our peace group is on the right track, those other groups are just kidding themselves." "You can only be for peace if you're anti-nuclear. Anyone who supports nuclear energy is obviously not for peace." Etc. Sometimes, in our zeal to create peace, we create win/lose battlegrounds that actually block the path to true peace.

Exercise

Can you think of an "Abe" in your life? Has there been someone in your life who has helped you to redefine your limited view of reality (your Tonal) into an expanded sense of the Nagual?

Write about this person here...

Chapter 3

What About Heroes?

"Please don't show our children Rambo."
Gennady A., Moscow, 1986

For one solid year, Diana and I had been working on this project that would blow the door off of Soviet-American citizen diplomacy. For an entire year, our proposal was countered by "Nyet" from the ministries of the Soviet bureaucracy. We were proposing to bring thirty teenagers from the USSR to the USA to live in the houses of American teenagers for one month, in order to live and play and study together. In this process of eating breakfast together, going to school together, exploring discos and pizza parlors and sandy beaches together, we knew that these young people would grow beyond the mistrust and fear of years of stereotyping on both sides. They would bond in friendship. If enough Soviet and American youths could do that then they would lead us all, in a few years, to a more harmonious world. But there must be a first, a precedent to begin the process and for a year they said NO. At least officially they said, "no."

I remember one meeting in Moscow when a Soviet official was loudly denouncing our plan, screaming, "Do you think we are fools to send the pride of our Soviet culture, our youth, to your crime-ridden, decadent, capitalist country?" There was a short break in the meeting. In the men's room, the Soviet official and I met again. Standing side by side, he leaned over to me and whispered in my ear, "Do you think my kid could go?"

Of course, getting him to say that in the meeting was another matter.

It was not until our informal network of friends in Moscow introduced me to Gennady Alferenko that we found a break in the frozen system. Gennady, a geophysicist and ballet dancer, is a man not afraid to put himself on the line for positive change. He is a true Warrior of the

Heart. He connected us to a leading figure in the Soviet Academy of Sciences and the NYET's began to change to DA.

**"Kids know, better than grownups, that
what we do is more important than what we say."**
Pete Seeger

After a year's worth of rejection, the approval came. After a full day and night of celebrating, Gennady took me to the airport. It was time for me to fly home and prepare to receive these Soviet teenagers, for the first time in history, into the homes and hearts of America. Gennady helped me with my luggage up to the customs control point. We embraced, tears flowing down both our faces. He kissed me on both cheeks and gave me a bear hug that only a Russian can give, then he grabbed me by my coat lapels and pulled my face to his. His voice cracking with emotion, he said, "Danaan, promise me something - promise me that you won't show our kids Rambo!"

I pulled back, startled and a bit amused. But his face told me this was no joke for him. I replied that I promised but, because my society was not as controlled as his was, I could not absolutely guarantee that no one would show it. But I would share his request with my co-workers. Satisfied, he hugged me again and I disappeared into that no-man's-land beyond passport control.

His comment stayed with me. Up at 30,000 feet, en route to Seattle, I began to ponder the reason why he had chosen to make that particular request as his final comment to me. He wasn't kidding and, as I allowed his words to sink in, I felt a depressing sadness settle over me. I asked myself, "Is this how the world sees us? Is this all that we export to the rest of the planet, this mindless violence in the guise of some superhero? Is Rambo really the best we can do; are there so many Americans who are so afraid of who they really are that they cut themselves off from their own inner darknesses and project that shadow out onto the world and call that grotesque figure their hero?"

I remembered a talk that I had given a year before in San Francisco. The title of my talk was "No More Gandhis." I remember that the title had drawn some criticism. Some-

one had said to me, "What do you mean, no more Gandhis? That's exactly what we need — someone to lead us, to inspire us, to show us the way." My response was that the time was passing wherein we could rely on superheroes to do it for us. The old way, that of setting up and following some charismatic leader and giving our power away to him or her, then blaming them for our faults, was no longer appropriate. There is a new way pushing on us, a way that is congruent with our evolution into the 21st century.

That new way is for you and me and thousands of us to free the Gandhi that lives within our own heart. That new way is to find the courage to unlock the Martin Luther King inside each of of us; to give birth to the Mother Theresa that is in each of our beings and to live that consciousness in our daily lives.

The answer then to the question, "Where are our new heroes?" is "*You* are our new hero and you and you and me and thousands of ordinary people just like you and me." These are our new heroes, and sheroes too, because the old patriarchal system of macho male war hero worship must change, and is changing, to a new awareness of leadership. This new style of leadership is a *shared* leadership, a grassroots leadership of thousands of women and men who know who they are, who own their own internal power for right action, and who are directing that power in the service of positive, peace-filled, non-violent human evolution.

I am talking about the Warrior of the Heart.

"For it isn't enough to talk about peace. One must believe in it.
And it isn't enough to believe in it. One must work at it."
Eleanor Roosevelt

Chapter 4

New Definitions for a New Way of Thinking

The way we define our world actually creates our world. Our words and concepts are incredibly powerful and you and I must become conscious of how we use them to create reality. John Wheeler, the Princeton physicist famous for his work with the sub-atomic nature of the Universe, said in 1973, "I think that through our own act of consciously choosing and posing questions about the Universe we bring about what we see taking place before us."

Remember the TONAL from the Yaqui Indians? Our definitions of "how it is" create the boundaries of the TONAL, our quite limited view of reality. When our definitions are open ended, they allow us to explore beyond our consentual TONAL out into the NAGUAL.

Exercise

Jot down a few of your definitions to give yourself a sense of your own power to create reality. How you define life is intimately connected to not only what you already have experienced, but also to what you will experience in the future.

What is your definition of:

SAFE:

CONFLICT:

PEACE:

ENEMY:

TRUTH:

I want you to know how I use words to create a new way of thinking about old, limited ideas. Here are some of the "re-definitions" that I use frequently in this book and in my life to help jog myself (and you) into looking at the "truth" with new, fresh eyes:

> **"Would that even today you *knew* the things that make for peace."**
> *The words of Jesus in Luke 19:42*

PEACE: The feeling tone in a SAFE-SPACE. A sense of harmony and "rightness" with one's environment. Differs markedly from the two old definitions of Peace:

Old Definition #1: Peace is an interim between wars. Peace is the opportunity to heal the wounded, bury the dead and sharpen our swords so we'll be ready for the next battle when it inevitably comes. (Obviously, this isn't "Peace" at all; it's just a lull in the cycles of the old war games. However, most governments define peace this way.)

Old Definition #2: Peace is some kind of blissful, mellow state which we may get to "someday." It's characterized by the words "nice" and "someday." We'll never get to it. Why? Because that's not who we human beings are. We're not always nice and mellow, we don't always agree, we do have conflicts. That has to be factored into our definition of peaceful or we'll just dream and wish our lives away trying to achieve some unattainable goal and keep killing each other because those "others" aren't fitting into our fantasy of what peace is supposed to look like. In fact, if we could achieve this mellow definition of Peace where we're all just hanging around in the hot tub of life being oh-so-nice and always agreeing on everything, I think we would all go nuts very quickly.

Humans need passion and challenge in their lives and any workable definition of peace must honor that fact. Real peace is an active, alive *process*. It's a verb, not a noun. It encompasses the inner feeling that you are just where you're supposed to be, doing what you were destined to do, in harmony with those around you who are doing what they were meant to do and in harmony with your planet.

Peace, the action-oriented verb, is happening when you and those around you are dealing with one another with respect, integrity and a sense of shared creativity. This can happen when you're meditating together or disagreeing in the midst of a heated meeting.

> **"Peace is neither the absence of war nor the presence of a disarmament agreement. Peace is a change of heart."**
>
> *Richard Lamm, former*
> *Governor of Colorado*

Note: This new definition of peace does not demand that you be necessarily quiet or "nice" or unconfused. In fact, this new, alive peace-full-ness can exist right in the midst of a conflict where you and your conflicted partner(s) may be yelling at each other. The difference is that, as you allow yourself to be immersed in the conflict, you also acknowledge "your truth" as relative and acknowledge the conflict as a productive process leading toward the best outcome for all and towards increased intimacy. To be peaceful in a conflict is to allow the energy of the conflict to take you and your partners to a greater understanding of your relationship.

CONFLICT: An opportunity for intimacy. An eruption of energy characterized by a deep feeling of hurt, resentment, loss, fear and a challenge to one's self-esteem. It is usually also characterized by the appearance of surface issues and demands that can be argued about (presenting problems) so that the deeper feelings (sourcing conflicts) won't have to be felt. (It never works!)

Conflict, when handled appropriately, can be a catalyst for increased awareness of ourselves and our connections to one another. It can be the crack in the hard shell of our persona that allows us to begin a journey to the center of our SELF.

POSITION: A strongly held belief, opinion or attitude as to "how it is" or "how it should be." An addiction to viewing a situation from only one angle. An expectation that there is only one way, one right outcome, one correct solution. A belief that truth is absolute and that you are the holder of that truth.

TRUTH: The way it is from your perspective and experience. Imagine that "THE" truth is inside a large box with several holes in it. "Your truth" is how *you* see this truth through one of the holes in the box. Other holes may yield different angles and different views of the same "truth".

SOURCING CONFLICT: What you're *really* in conflict about. The underlying source of the dispute. The *hurt* and/or resentment and/or fear that is too real and/or terrifying and/or "wrong" to admit to. Sourcing conflicts are usually related to issues of self-esteem, abandonment, unworthiness, guilt, psychological security, sexuality or failure. Sourcing conflicts almost always are related to issues about *intimacy* and are usually rooted in childhood.

PRESENTING PROBLEM: The surface issues and disagreement in a conflicted situation that mask the "sourcing conflict" which must be dealt with for real resolution to occur. Typically, *whatever* you are arguing about in a prolonged conflict is a presenting problem. We invent presenting problems immediately to shield ourselves from addressing the real, and usually very threatening, sourcing conflict.

WIN/WIN: A solution that meets the needs (not necessarily "wants") of all concerned. An outcome that allows each person involved to feel that they were listened to, respected and included as an equal partner in the decision. Win/win is an outcome of approaching a conflict as a "shared opportunity for growth," as an "interdependent challenge requiring co-creating and teamwork." Win/win happens when all parties are willing to embark on a journey of exploration beyond the "presenting problem" all the way to the discovery of the "real conflict."

PRESENTING PROBLEMS/SOURCE CONFLICTS

When you hear someone who must *blame* (who can I sue; she's at fault, if it wasn't for them, etc.) or play *victim* (I can't do it; it's not worth it; I'll never get it right) or *project* (she's the angry one, not me; when they stop being so stupid I'll listen to them; you can't trust a ____, etc.) ... then stop and ask yourself "what is the *source conflict* that lies underneath the *presenting problems?*"

When people begin to take responsibility for their own feelings and actions and see their own part in the "dance of conflict" (when they move beyond "blame") then they can discover the deeper *source conflict* that *the presenting problem* is masking. Below are some Source Conflicts which are only "possibly connected" to the Presenting Problems opposite them. There are many possibilities.

Presenting Problems (the conflicts we *think* we're fighting about.)	**Source Conflicts** (the deeper conflicts that must be addressed)
There's never enough money, she/he always wants more. I'm sick of being responsible for everything.	I only feel loved for what I can do, not what I am. I don't want to have to *earn* someone's love.
She/He doesn't care about me anymore.	I never feel really listened to; never really valued.
My opinion doesn't count around here.	There is no trust left in this relationship.
I want custody of the kids.	I'm deeply hurt and if I show it I'll get hurt some more.
I'm so angry that I can't even talk about it.	I feel out of control.
I demand a legal settlement.	I feel like I have no power here.
She/He wants too much from me.	I don't know how to be intimate.

When we only deal with others at the level of the presenting problem, we get stuck in win/lose, right/wrong, good/bad. When we're stuck in presenting problems, then there's never enough to go around and so win/win is not possible. The best we can do is "compromise".

Only when we get down to the source conflict can we begin to collaborate about win/win solutions. Here there *is* enough to go around, and intimacy is possible "us against the problem" instead of "me against you".

SAFE: Not requiring protection. Open and vulnerable due to lack of need for protection. In harmony with one's surroundings; in context with the whole.

SAFE SPACE: A physical and psychological environment wherein everyone in that environment feels safe. A place wherein you and everyone present can explore options and alternatives. An environment wherein "positions" have been temporarily laid aside and where the exploration of "win/win" outcomes is possible.

Note: "Safety in this safe-space may not feel like the old definition of safe. In fact, it could feel scary and/or challenging because we are giving ourselves permission to look at and lay aside our positions. Safe spaces feel alive and growth-filled. They are places to take risks, to experiment with new ways of thinking and being."

2
LOOKING INWARD

Chapter 5

How Our Heads Work

On the way to becoming a Warrior of the Heart, you will be asked to experience many things, some of which may seem silly or even a bit crazy. These experiences will help you to upgrade years and years of cultural programming that, in effect, has taught you that you do not have a peaceful, positive, powerful Warrior within you. You must override this deeply ingrained programming before you will be able to allow new, really new information to set you free.

Let's take a tour through your head. There are some internal mechanisms at work in your brain that you must understand on your path to deeper awareness.

Let's first discuss the Medulla, the oldest section of your brain. The medulla (animal brain) was with us long before we humans decided to get off all fours and stand up on two legs. This ancient brain sits right on top of your spinal column and essentially directs the flow of traffic, the information that many of your senses are reporting on. The medulla acts like a traffic cop, deciding which information will get through to the central processing unit, the cerebral cortex, and which will not.

Recent research tells us that only about 30% of the information coming to us at any moment actually makes it through the medulla to the cerebral cortex, where it only then becomes conscious, available for processing and decision-making. The other 70% (that's right, 70%) gets shunted off into our unconscious. Our conscious mind is never aware that the information was ever there. The bulk of the data impinging on us at every moment simply is not allowed into our reality-set (our tabletop, our Tonal, as the Yaqui would put it).

Now, if you've really been working on your consciousness for years, then maybe 35% gets through, but no more. This means that most of the people of the world are making decisions, forming judgments, drawing deep, meaningful conclusions based on, at most, 35% of the information available to accurately, consciously run their lives. Embedded in that 70% or 65%

of "lost" information are certainly large pieces of the puzzle which are needed to make clear decisions and form accurate judgments about what's right, what's wrong, who's good, who's bad, etc.

The most important question about all this is, "On what basis does the medulla let through some information and exclude most of it?" What criteria does the medulla use to decide what will and won't exist in your tabletop reality?" While we're not sure about the answer, we can make some educated guesses based upon the overall function that the medulla plays and has played for thousands of years. Remember, it's the oldest brain in you, the one that helped to save your life from lions and tigers outside the cave, the brain that helped you decide at a very rudimentary level whether you should attack or flee that hairy thing lurking in the forest. It is the brain that accepts central nervous system alarm bells and says whether flight or fight response will increase chances of survival this time. It makes decisions based on survival; primal, physical survival.

Said in a little looser manner, you are being fed 30% of the available information in your world and you're being fed it by a caveman brain that runs on survival or fear.

Part of the path of the Warrior of the Heart is the re-training of your medulla, so that it lets through much more of the 70% of presently unavailable information (you can handle *incredible* amounts of information in your cerebral cortex, it's just sitting there waiting). Even more importantly, the path of the Warrior of the Heart is the re-training of the medulla so that it re-programs the bases upon which it makes its decisions as to what gets through and what goes directly into your unconscious. It is possible to re-train your brain away from decisions made by fear of annihilation, away from "me against you" survival, and towards "me and you" survival and the co-creation of a better world for all. But it won't just happen because it's a nice idea. The Warrior must commit her or himself to this path as a model for others.

Okay, let's go a little further and look at what happens to that 30% or 35% of the information that *does* get through your medulla. This information now enters your cerebral cortex, the part of your brain wherein you become conscious of the information's existence. This is the part of your brain where the decisions get made. So at least the information that made it to the cortex is available for clear decision-making and for the integration of new, higher quality behavior, right? Wrong.

It seems that our conscious brain, the cortex, compares every piece of new information to every piece of old information in our head. The cerebral cortex doesn't handle new information very well, I'm afraid. It's as if you had a roladex file in your head or a large stack of 3" x 5" cards. On these 3" x 5" cards is written every piece of information, every experience, every feeling, thought and scenario that has ever entered the cortex since it was a cortex (maybe even before!). When a new piece of information comes in, it is immediately compared to every piece of old information on the stack of 3" x 5" cards. Your brain is looking for a *match*, a close comparison, so it can say, "Aha, I know how to handle this, why I'll just file it on card 1,312...."

Have you ever said something like, "Boy, he really reminds me of _____?" Or, you're driving through a spectacular pass between two mountain ranges with a brilliant sunset flooding the car and you say, "This reminds me of _____."

Your cerebral cortex is madly flipping through its stack of 3" x 5" cards trying to get a comparison, trying to make a match of this newness with something already in the 3" x 5" card stack. It *will* find a match. It *will* tear that newness apart and cram it on to one of those damn old 3" x 5" cards so it (you) can make "sense" out of your world.

Unfortunately, there is no 3" x 5" card that pops up and says, "STOP! Do not cram this information on an old card. This is totally new information." There is no mechanism in our brains that allows new information to remain new, fresh, alive. It gets torn apart and filed into an already existing category.

Some wit has said that our twentieth century culture is suffering from an epidemic disease called "hardening of the categories." Right on.

So, we have uncovered another task of the Warrior of the Heart. We need to insert that new 3" x 5" card into our pile of cards - one that says, "STOP! *Breathe*, appreciate the newness of this moment, the uniqueness of this awareness, the aliveness and specialness of this situation." To re-train your brain to permit newness to live within you is one of the most precious gifts you can give to yourself and to every being on our planet, it will happen for you as you walk the path of the Heart Warrior. Celebrate. A word of caution: to follow this path, to allow newness in your life, you will be asked to travel far beyond the *Tonal* where things have to "make sense." Are you willing to surrender your death-grip on your neatly filed sensible world?

Exercise: Filtered Information

You know that your Medulla is filtering information
based on its need to survive its "boogey-man"
world, when you begin to think or feel:

> Nobody likes me.
> I'm stupid.
> I can't do it.
> They won't love me if...
> I can't make a mistake.
> I've got to win.
> I'm a loser.
> I'm powerless.
> What difference can I make?
> Who cares what I think (feel)?
> I've always got to be on guard.
> I'll probably get sick.
> I don't deserve ____.
> They're out to get me.
> There isn't enough to go around.
> Get them before they get you.

**Fill in some of your own personal "medulla
messages" that keep you at the 35% level:**

Exercise: Upgrade and Reprogram

When you feel your Medulla limiting your
access to life, try these re-programmers to
allow more and better information to flow to
your "dot connecting" cerebral cortex:

> I love myself.
> I am wise.
> I can DO it.
> I am 100% lovable.
> My mistakes are my teachers.
> I just have to be true to me.
> I deserve the best.
> I'm a powerful peacemaker.
> I can change the world by changing me.
> The world needs my gifts.
> This is a friendly Universe.
> My life is my gift to us all.
> Health is my natural state.
> I nourish life and life nourishes me.
> I create my life.
> There is enough for all of that which
> really matters.
> Every living being is a part of my family.

**Fill in your own personal "re-programmers" to
open up the flow within you:**

Chapter 6

Getting to Know Your SELF

I Commit To Peace
Bring The Enemy Without, Within;
Within, Without

Franklin

Large Round Persona
Is Masquerading Shadow
Smothering The Self

Pat

The SELF

I have alluded to the SELF when I said that, if your power comes from your connection to your SELF instead of from your position, you can allow yourself to relinquish your need to be *right* at all costs. To understand the idea of your SELF, let's look at a simple model from Jungian psychology, which portrays the individual as a sphere, made up of layers and layers of awareness and experience.

The outermost layer of the sphere is called the *Persona*. In this layer are all of your personality traits, all of your credentials and successes that you like to show to others. Everything in our Persona is true, it's just that we have found through experience that when we let people see what is in our Persona, they usually will like us for it. And so, when I first meet a person or a group of people, I show them my Persona. "Hello, there," I say, "I'm Danaan Parry and I have these impressive credentials and I've travelled to all these countries and I'm successful at these things, etc. etc." And my little boy inside hopes that you will like me, accept me, affirm me. We *all* have Personas.

As we look below the Persona, the outermost layer of "who-we-are," we find many inner layers. These are the accumulation of the many years of "acculturation," of learning how to survive,

how to fit into a society with definite rules of behavior and
severe psychological penalties for *not* fitting in.

One of the most important inner layers is the *Shadow*. Just as
the Persona contains all those things about us that we want the
world to see, the *Shadow* layer contains all those things about
us that we *do not* want anyone to see. Our years of acculturation
have taught us, usually painfully, that there are certain facets of
our nature, certain emotions and ways of being that if discovered, will cause us to experience rejection, disapproval and
even hostility from others. We get taught by bitter experience
that "it's not okay to be that way." So we try to change who we
are, not by honoring and working with these ways-of-being, but
by stuffing them down, pushing them inside, hoping that they
will go away. And they never do. Just as conflict never goes
away by simply pretending it isn't there when it is, so too these
"negative" feelings and behaviors don't disappear when we
lock them up inside us. They go down to the layer of the *Shadow*
and accumulate there, like the hot molten lava within the earth.
Sadly, the more we push down and try to ignore our "non-
acceptable" side, the more power we give it. For many people it
results in their Shadow running their life. They spend most of
their available energy trying to hide their not-okayness and
everyone sees it but them.

My years of counselling have taught me that, at a level of
consciousness just below our surface consciousness, we *all
know about each other*. In other words, at the surface or Persona
level of social relationships we pretend not to know about each
other, but in fact we all have incredible, intuitive sensing
mechanisms and it's really impossible to hide ourselves from
anyone, especially those who love us. There will come a day
when enough people feel good enough about themselves and
about experiencing deep intimacy with others, and on that day
we will collectively open up our Personas and admit that it's
okay to know, really know each other. Until then, the bulk of
humanity will go on pretending that we are separate, isolated
entities and that we really can hide ourselves from one another.
And a small handful of people will have the courage to see, and
admit they see, beyond the illusion.

That brings us to the *SELF*, the very center of the sphere-that-
is-you or me. This can be a confusing word because different
psychological disciplines use this word for different aspects of

the psyche. Here, from Jungian psychology, I define the *SELF* as that core of you, that place at the center of your being where you know who you are, where you know, unequivocally, that you are whole and complete and that you are *love*. Here, at the *SELF*, lives that clear being that has nothing to prove, does not have to *earn* love, because it *is* love.

You may recognize a distinct difference between this definition of what lies at your center and the theologies of some major religious belief systems. In the religion that I was raised in, I was told that my center was a weak, prone-to-evil soul that could only be saved by the good graces of the church. It was a powerful control mechanism called "original sin" which declared that I came into this life less-than-whole and needed the church to make me whole.

But here Carl Jung says that our center is whole, clear, love. It is the layer upon layer of accumulated sophistication that keeps us from remembering this truth and leaves us susceptible to the guilt-trips and seductions of outer belief systems.

Jung said something else that isn't picked up by many contemporary writers. For me it is the most valuable piece of wisdom in Jungian psychology, because it speaks to who we really are, at the level of the *SELF*. Let me explain it in my own way of feeling it:

Most of us humans spend most of our lives "bouncing-off of" each other's Personas. Whether it's a one-time encounter or a marriage of forty years, most of us are like billiard balls on a table, bouncing off each other's outer shells and not allowing anyone to really penetrate below this surface layer. (I do believe that everyone, some time in their lifetime, has the experience of having their sphere penetrated, so that deeper layers are revealed. For most, this experience is so terrifying that they immediately bring all their forces to bear so as to "heal" the breech of security and the Persona quickly closes over the exposed inner levels, leaving a thick scar tissue to prevent further incursions.)

But every once in awhile, someone has the courage, or the situation forces us, to touch at a deeper level and stay there for awhile. We can then discover the rewards of this "inner journey." We discover for the first time how good it feels to feel. I mean *really* feel, not pretend-feel like most people do when they *think* they feel. Thinking feelings has become a great American pastime, and movements like growth groups and the new age are full of it.

It is the experience of this authentic feeling-state, with its sense of "finally I've come home," or at least "I'm on my way home at last," that hooks us, compels us to continue our journey deeper and deeper to the center of our SELF. Even when we hit the layer of the *Shadow* with all its "scaries" and old anger, its feelings of not-okayness and un-lovableness, we somehow recognize that we are finally facing how-it-is at this level, instead of more pretend-how-it-is games. And the truth is so compelling, integrity so refreshing, that we find the will to look our Shadows right in the eye, right in the mirror, and discover the teddy bear hiding behind the fierce dragon.

Onward we go, deeper, until the moment comes (usually after becoming lost for awhile) when we experience what the Christian mystics called "the dark night of the soul." You give up and acknowledge that you're okay just the way you are. And then it's there, a glimpse usually, a brief experience of the *SELF*. And what is it? Beyond the words I have already used to describe it, there is one point about your *SELF* that contains the exciting revelation (or rather deep remembering) of who and what we truly are. And it only comes in relationships. That is when you reveal your-*SELF* to me and I reveal my *SELF* to you, we discover that my-*SELF* and your *SELF* are the same *SELF*.

There is only one SELF. It is our point of oneness, of total connection. At this deepest level of who we are, we are one. All the other layers are where the differences, the uniqueness and the separation are. Both are true. We are a paradox. At the same moment we are both totally unique from any other being and also totally connected, one, with every other being. It seems that our awareness of our different-ness comes quite easily and that our awareness (or our remembering) of our oneness is the result of our journey of awakening; a journey that is worth whatever price one must pay. It is perhaps the only true journey one can make. And it is surely the journey of the Warrior of the Heart.

Exercise

It's healthy to look at ourselves in terms of our "layers" to discover what we put where. Please jot down some words in the three areas of PERSONA, SHADOW and SELF on this page. Perhaps you will also come up with other layers that describe other depths of "who you are." For instance, you might put your *name* under PERSONA because it feels like only a surface connection to you. Or you might be moved to put it down deeper, maybe between the PERSONA and the SHADOW, because your name expresses deeper parts of you. Where will you put your gender word: man or woman? Where will you put your profession? Your family connection (husband, wife, lover, daughter, son, father, mother)?

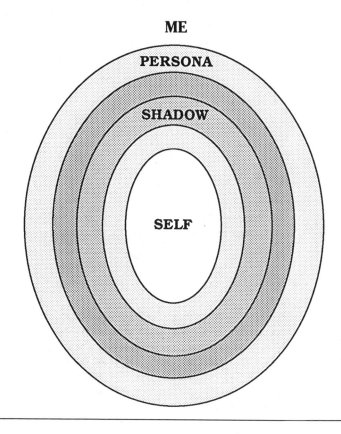

ME

PERSONA

SHADOW

SELF

Exercise

Now fill this out for your FATHER (or whoever you feel filled that role in your life). Some words may be the same as in yours; some will be very different. Just close your eyes for a few moments and call his image to you. Then open your eyes and let the words flow onto the areas of his sphere where they belong.

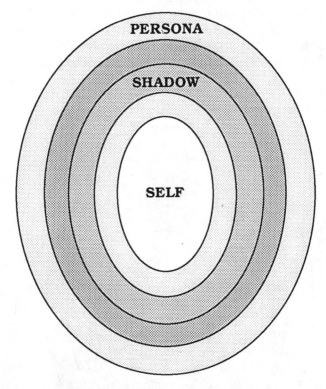

MY FATHER

PERSONA

SHADOW

SELF

Remember, you are doing this about another person, not yourself. In actuality, we cannot ever really describe another person, only the image of that person that we have in our minds. It's like looking into that "box" labelled TRUTH. Someone looking through another peephole on another side would see a different reality. Remember that this is *your* picture, not THE picture, and as such tells you more about *you* than about anyone else.

Exercise

Now do one for your MOTHER (or whoever filled that role in your life). Again, close your eyes and call to you the image of your Mother. Then open your eyes and start filling in the layers.

MY MOTHER

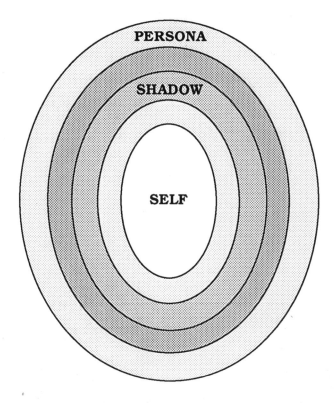

PERSONA

SHADOW

SELF

Of course, the same is true here. This gives you information about how *You* see your world. It's that old saying that "what we say about others says more about us than about them." There is great learning for us in this.

Exercise

Now it's time to do one about your Lover. I use the word lover to mean the one person in your life who fills the role of Primary Relationship. If there is no one who now fills that role in your life, choose someone who is the closest person to you right now.

MY LOVER

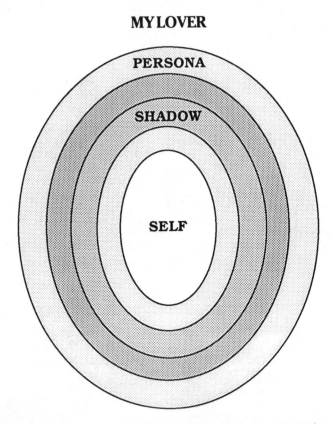

It is important to consider sharing this information with the three people that you have created these images for. This is especially true for this one about your lover. I recommend that you "create a safe space" and invite this person to listen to you share your image of them while acknowledging that this says more about *you* than them. You might ask this person to create a sphere of you, too.

Chapter 7

Aloneness
Your Power Spot

Starry, Frigid Night
Stark, Alone With Fears As Friends
Warrior Of The Heart

Hardy

"...there is a pervasive form of contemporary violence to
which the idealist fighting for peace by nonviolent
methods most easily succumbs: activism and overwork.
The rush and pressure of modern life are a form, perhaps
the most common form, of its innate violence. To allow
oneself to be carried away by a multitude of conflicting
concerns, to surrender to too many demands, to commit
oneself to too many projects, to want to help everyone in
everything is to succumb to violence. More than that, it is
cooperation in violence. The frenzy of the activist
neutralizes his work for peace. It destroys his own inner
capacity for peace. It destroys the fruitfulness of his own
work, because it kills the root of inner wisdom which
makes work fruitful.

Thomas Merton

There are three very different states of being that few people
understand and that get lumped together into one big pile. The
pile is usually given a negative connotation. These three states
are:

Alone
Lonely
Aloneness

They are *not even close* to one another and, in fact, the state of
being I refer to as Aloneness is a positive, powerful state where
the Warrior of the Heart lives.

I was 34 years old before I even experienced the state of
Alone. *I grew up with my mother or aunts always around to*

make my decisions for me. Then I went straight into the U.S. Coast Guard which was another "mommie" to take care of me. While in the Coast Guard I married and, being a fairly traditional marriage, I was again "taken care of" by my wife. When my marriage collapsed after twelve years, I found to my complete terror that I was now alone *for the first time in my life.*

My initial response, clearly a "fight or flight" survival technique straight from my Medulla, was what is euphemistically called "sport-screwing." Dozens of lonely nights in dozens of bars, picking up dozens of lonely women who were just as frightened as I was to face being alone. Those few months of frenetic denial were the most painful and the most lonely times in my life. I found out that the deepest form of loneliness happens when you're in a crowd or in bed with another lonely person.

I said, "Okay, being alone can't be any worse than this loneliness I feel while I'm avoiding being alone, so let's see what Alone *is really like." I guess I'm the kind of person who needs to get hit over the head with a 2 x 4 to get his own attention and so I moved out of my buddy's apartment and bought a boat. What a boat! It was an old Navy LCVP, a landing craft used in World War II; you know, the one where the front flops down on the beach and John Wayne comes running out, his rifle blazing. Some old riverboat captain had converted it into a tugboat/houseboat. I met him in a bar in Antioch, California. Two hours and ten beers later, he had $2000 of mine and I had the SEAJAY. God help me.*

I scrubbed the diesel fuel off that old hulk for a week, moved in my stuff and rented a slip at the Bethel Island Marina. I was the only "live-aboard." I'd drive there after work, untie the SEAJAY and motor out into the San Juaquin Channel. I'd tie up to a buoy and spend the night out there in the blackness of the Sacramento River. I was Alone.

For the first two weeks, my mind played every trick on me it could. I would fantasize about every woman I had ever slept with. I would wake up in the middle of the night and tear through every box and cabinet on the boat looking for something to read, some book to take my mind off of being Alone. I made phone calls in my head, wrote

*letters in my head to every person I ever knew, made up
songs — God, I was scared to look inside.*
*But, in my aloneness, the "inside" came out to look at
me. After a while, I stopped fighting. Night after night, I
would sit on the aft deck of that old boat in the darkness
with only the rubbing of the boat against the buoy as a
sound. Night after night, the demons and dragons came to
be with me. At first, I wrestled with them in mortal combat;
then, I stopped wrestling and just watched them, acknowledged them. I began to look forward to them. I gave them
names. We became friends. The night became my ally, not
my enemy.*

Somehow, slowly, I had moved from *lonely* to *alone*. Lonely
was disempowering. I was lonely with people and lonely *without*
people. Alone was better. But, for awhile, until I stopped fighting
it, *Alone* was also disempowering. As long as Alone wasn't okay,
it was my Master and a terrifying one.

But, just as *lonely* had shifted to *alone; alone*, after I surrendered to it, began to shift to yet something else, something
deeper and calmer.

Aloneness

There comes a time after you have stopped all the frantic
games of *persona* to *persona* surface relating, after you have
surrendered to your being *alone* and have let the demons and
dragons come out of your shadow and have learned to dance
with them. There comes a time when ...

... the bullshit just stops ... and *there you are.*

I cannot possibly describe this in words. It's *something* like,
"Oh, so *this* is what's real" or "Oh, now I get it." Or, you just start
laughing and laughing and you don't *understand* why but you
know why. Here you are. All the stuff falls away; all the ferocious,
evil demons have names like Hank and Cibyl and are funny, little
furry things and you are totally alone in the Universe and it's
okay. In fact, it's *great!* Alone has transformed from "poor-me-
weak" to "yummy-powerful." Of *course* you are alone, each of us
is alone. We come together to nourish, heal, support and
empower each other but, ultimately, we are all alone. We are
always in that space between trapezes and that is a place of
Aloneness. Cherish it.

I meet people all the time who have lived alone for years, yet they have never surrendered to it, have never befriended it, have never extracted the power from it and made it their ally. They have never known ALONENESS.

There is a way for you to explore that positive, powerful state called *Aloneness* and I ask that you consider it because it holds much learning and strength for you. It is a giant step on your path of the Warrior of the Heart.

No, you don't have to dissolve all your relationships and move onto a boat or join a monastery. You may need to go on what is called a Vision Quest.

VISION QUEST

Now watch the pictures forming in your minds and the dots connecting about what I'm talking about. Just relax and let me tell you about what I mean by the words Vision Quest.

A Vision Quest requires four elements:

> You
> Nature
> Time
> Aloneness

That's it. Simple, huh? Simple, yes; easy, no. Mostly, for folks like you and me, the biggest hurdle is Time. This isn't going to fit into your "Daily Planner" between meetings. But, it probably won't take weeks, either, unless you want it to.

Start planning it and just see what happens. Where will you do it? It must be a place of wildness and quiet. It could be a deserted beach somewhere or an alpine meadow or a redwood forest or ???

Leave the books and magazines home and the trinkets, crystals and "special things," too. No phone. Nothing to "keep you busy." Busy is the enemy. Boredom is your tool. That's right, embrace boredom. When it comes, welcome it, wallow in it; it is your bridge to the other side. Walk in nature. Listen to the water. Feel the wind. Be bored. Be alone.

When alone feels good and boredom feels just fine, when all the old movies in your head have played themselves to death and the old fantasies are just oatmeal, just smile. (You'll know what I mean when you get there.) Aloneness.

I wish that there were some way to have you not read the

following words until you have reached the point of fully embracing aloneness on your Vision Quest. But, what the heck.

When you have reached the state of Aloneness, you can ask questions about yourself and about "how it is" that you could not ask before. Why? Because, if you have truly embraced Aloneness, you are in the Nagual. Prior to that, all your questions, and your answers, come from the Tonal. Prior to Aloneness, you are just piling on more old movie scripts on to the same old tabletop of limited, consentual reality. Nothing really new. From the Nagual, from the Point of Aloneness, you can see what is New.

So, now it's time to look at you as Warrior. It's time to ask some questions. It's time to go out to the car, open the trunk, lift up the spare tire and pull out this book which you have hidden until now, or it's time to dig down into the bottom of your backpack, down under the spare wool socks and trail-mix, to get to this book which you have *not* used on your Vision Quest to keep you from being bored. You wipe the granola stains off of it, open it and turn to each of the pages where you have written about yourself and others.

When you stop laughing, write some new stuff from where you are now, from the Nagual.

Then read the section called *The Warrior in the Meadow* and complete the drawing of yourself as the Warrior in the Meadow on the following pages.

The Warrior in the Meadow

Picture yourself in a lush, green meadow. It is springtime and all about you are the new wildflowers. The yellows, blues, pinks and whites dazzle your eyes as they create a waving blanket of wild color across the forest meadow.

Then you become aware of yourself. You are dressed in the traditional garments of your heritage. The colors that you wear are symbolic of not only the lineage of your tribe but also your unique place in your culture today. As you survey your attire, you see that you have carefully chosen to wear certain symbols and objects of meaning to you. Some of them have been passed down to you by your mother and represent her gifts to you. Those are your connection to her and also her connection to her lineage. Some of the symbols and objects have been passed down to you by your father and are his gifts to you and your connection to his lineage. Other symbols and objects have been given to you by other significant people in your life (grandparent, aunt, uncle, brother, sister, lover, friend, child, etc.). Still others are yours alone, earned by you or mysteriously given to you by the universe.

As you stand alone in this lush, life-filled natural setting, you are aware that you have donned the garment and raiment of the new Warrior, today's Samarai. You are, at the same moment, the here-and-now representative of hundreds, perhaps thousands, of years of heritage with lines of energy that thread their way back to your father's father's father's father's father and to your mother's mother's mother's mother's mother - and - you are also a unique, fresh, brand-new being, full of new awareness and new information never before available on this earth.

Our planet needs you to be the Warrior of the Heart; totally aware of both your ancient heritage and your newness, your potential. As you stand in that meadow, you *are* these things, 100%.

Exercise

THE WARRIOR IN THE MEADOW

I ask you now to take a few minutes to draw yourself. It can be a very worthwhile exercise. The you I want you to sketch is that Warrior of the Heart in you. It will help you to re-member, to re-connect with the deep symbols and energies within you that will facilitate the awakening of your Heart Warrior. My own symbol is the soaring eagle with a big heart on it. I have colors, garments, trinkets and sacred objects (sacred to me because of who has given them to me or the events surrounding their being given). Now it's time for you to identify your own.

With your eyes closed, imagine yourself in your Warrior garments and become aware of your colors, your choice of designs and fabrics, how the various elements blend and harmonize.

Become aware of the ritual objects you have chosen to adorn you, the sacred jewelry you wear, the symbols sewn in or attached to your garments. What are these symbols?

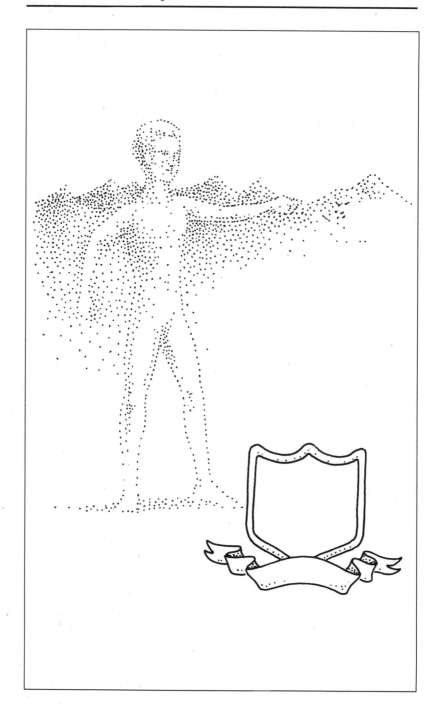

When you open your eyes, begin sketching clothing on the page provided using a pencil. Don't be intimidated because you can't figure out how to make a cape look right or how to correctly draw a shirt or a blouse. Have fun with it. Erase a line here and try it over there. Notice not just what symbols come to you but also where you choose to arrange them. Use whatever symbols come to you. How is your hair combed/arranged? Do you wear anything on your head?

In the lower corner of the drawing, I have placed a shield. This is your Warrior of the Heart "coat of arms" except that it's not a shield to protect you from anyone and the "arms" aren't weapons, they are arms for reaching out to others. These are "arms for hugging." It is here on this page so that you can sketch your own Heart Warrior symbol or symbols. What are they? (Perhaps none come immediately but now you have asked, you have knocked on the door of your own subconscious and the answer will come in its own time.)

Notice that below your shield is a "scroll" for you to write some saying or motto that expresses in words (left brain) what your drawing (right brain) depicts symbolically.

Draw in a wild animal or bird at your side. This is your totem, your power animal. Don't think about what being should be at your side, just draw it. Draw in an object in your outstretched hand. It might be a staff, a sword, a wand, a pole, a spear, a cup, whatever. Just draw it.

Put the book away. Return to nature, to Aloneness. You will know when it's time to go home.

Going home is as important as being in aloneness. The act of creating aloneness is not done for itself. It is a tool for unlocking clarity and stillness, calm and centeredness in the Heart Warrior. All these the Warrior brings back to his/her life in the world. All these the Warrior shares freely just as the Yaqui Warrior ventures into the Nagual and brings back newness and change to the tribal Tonal. The Warrior's quest is not complete until the Tonal has expanded for the whole tribe.

In other words, don't use Aloneness as a place to hide. Use it as a place to gather gifts to share.

Your Power Spot

There is a valuable "tool" that should be in the "tool kit" of every Warrior of the Heart whether she is a Chief Executive Officer of a major corporation or he is a full-time single parent of six kids (or both). This tool is your Power Spot.

Your Power Spot is a place in nature where you can relatively easily, tap back into your Aloneness. It's a natural setting that holds for you the qualities of calm, quiet, wild, earthy, grounded, centered. It is for you only. If the place where you discovered ALONENESS is far away, you'll have to find another, closer place.

The elements necessary for your Power Spot are:

- You can get to it fairly easily (it can't be hours away; you should be able to reach it, spend a few hours there and get back easily in a day at most).

- It must be a natural setting. (Elemental energies must be readily available and they are not with concrete around.)

- It must be reasonably unpopulated by humans. (You need to have a good probability of being quite alone there. This does not exclude wild animals, of course, just humans and their trappings of "civilization.")

- It must say to you "here I am, I'm what you're looking for." (Initially, you will have to "go looking" but, in your wandering through the woods or along a creek or down a beach, it will find you. Take lots of time to wander with your intellect turned down and your intuition turned up. Explore varied environments. You'll know.)

- It needs to be "its own place." This means that it should be somehow defined; it should feel "self-contained." For example, not a long, unbroken stretch of beach but maybe an inlet or a rock outcropping; not a whole hillside but maybe a nook or a turn in a stream or a small grove of trees that feel "connected."

- You need to "claim" it. Your Power Spot is just for you. Respect that. No matter how great a spot it is, resist the urge to bring your lover there or your kids, etc. Keep your own energy field there and keep it clear. Consider placing a thing of value to you under a stone or in a nook of a tree.

You do not own this place but, if it is your Power Spot, then the Nature forces there will blend with you in a win-win sharing. It's okay to be selfish about your Power Spot and not share it with other humans.

Why does the Warrior need a Power Spot?

You know the value of being grounded and centered. You know about slowing down and learning to *listen*. You know about going within to transform the shadow on your journey to the SELF. You have also tasted the power of Aloneness.

Your Power Spot is a place for you to RE-MEMBER, literally. You go to your Power Spot to re-connect with the *magic* within you and in nature. It reawakens your sense of wonder, your awe at the incredible beauty of it all, even the beauty of the dance of conflict.

Find your Power Spot. Claim it. Use it often. It is at your Power Spot that you will hear that calm, clear inner voice; the voice that always tells you truth. Listen.

You may wish to insert a photo, map, or drawing of your power spot here.

Chapter 8

Reclaiming Our Darkness

Darkness. The Chill Fire
Of My Soul Always Goes Out
Unless I Feed It.

Bob

"Oneness isn't necessarily nice"

Melting the Borders that Divide Us

There's an experience that I had a couple of years ago in Northern Ireland that "made real" many of the concepts I am now sharing with you. I had been asked by a number of peace groups to facilitate a meeting between the heads of two warring factions, one Catholic and one Protestant, to try and get some communication flowing. The peace groups were successful in getting an agreement from the leaders of these two opposing paramilitary organizations. That agreement was only to come to this meeting and sit in the room, nothing more.

For three days I facilitated this meeting. For three days, the people sat there. That's it, they just sat there. Nothing happened. It was like a morgue in that room. I used every trick in the book, every skill I had, to get them to talk to each other. Nothing. These leaders of armed camps whose followers were sworn to kill one another just glared and scowled and muttered one-liners to their lieutenants. All of Thursday and Friday and Saturday I worked, they scowled and we went nowhere!

But then it's Sunday and everything stops in Ireland on Sunday. We, too, took the day off and I got a promise from the two sides that they would show up Monday morning and we would try again.

Before we left, I asked the leader of the Protestant organization for permission to do a walking tour through his area to get to know it and the people better. He agreed and suggested two things. Dress like an American (which means a bit too gaudy) and take along someone who would be recognized as friendly to the politics of the area, the Shankill district. I chose a female friend who was a local social worker.

The Shankill district is one of the Protestant ghettos of Belfast. It is separated from the Catholic ghettos by what is now a scarred, partially burned-out no-person land of two to three blocks. It stands as a sad testament to hundreds of years of hatred. Something in me knows that I must understand all this if I am to be more than another "expert," another voyeur in this troubled land.

So, we walk the streets of the Shankill. Sun shines on hastily painted graffiti demanding the release of the H-Block Seven. Children play at guerrilla warfare in bombed-out shops. Ahead of us, a young mother pushes her baby carriage and life goes on.

Suddenly, swiftly, from behind us, a British Army armored personnel carrier appears and stops right next to us. The heavy metal hatch of the vehicle clanks open and now there are four British soldiers, boys it seems, with machine guns. One has his gun stuck in my ribs, one has his pointed at my friend, one is pointing his weapon at the young mother and the fourth scans the rooftops ready to open fire on any would-be sniper.

A British officer emerges from the armored vehicle. His thin, tight, fully uniformed frame steps to the mother. He clicks his heels, tips his hat to her, then reaches into the baby carriage. With one hand, he raises the baby and, with the other, he searches the carriage. The baby struggles and screams in one hand while he pulls apart the lining of the baby carriage with the other hand looking for hidden weapons or explosives. Satisfied, the officer places the baby back in the carriage and covers it with the remnants of the torn lining. He clicks his heels and, with another doff of the hat, he is back in his steel machine. The soldiers quickly follow and then they are gone. All this takes no more than two minutes.

Now the mother is out in the middle of the street, crouched low in some primal position, screaming from hundreds of years of resentment. Over and over, she screams at the disappearing dot of armored vehicle, "Bloody British bastards, you bloody British bastards!" Her energy washes over me like a giant wave.

Now I am out in the street and I am screaming. Somehow, I have plugged into the rage, the hatred, the fear and I am screaming from a place so deep in me that it feels ancient and cellular and very, very dark. With that small part of my rational mind that is still functioning, I am aware that I would like to cause pain to something, anything! Then it is over. I am looking at the young mother, she at me. Her baby cries. The sun shines.

I am aware of only two things. One, the surface thought, is that this is very hard on my ego image of who-I-am. Here's this hot-shot conflict resolution expert from the States come to help these folks and he's out in the street engulfed in primal rage.

The other awareness, much deeper, is that as I look at the young Irish mother, I am feeling a connection with her that is so intimate, so pure, that the boundaries between us are dissolving. I look at the baby and my friend, and I am experiencing a totality of connection with them now, beyond ego, that can only be described as that oneness state that I, for years, have only talked and lectured about but never really experienced. All of the walls, all of the protection borders that I had erected for all those years, they are crumbling and I am left in total communion, at-one with these people. And, as I stare down the street, I am aware that I feel this same intimate connection with those soldiers, that British officer. My God, I don't want to feel a oneness with that officer. But I do. I feel him, know him, as me. I feel his pain, his fear, his isolation. And, I feel mine. We are one, beyond any trite idea of what that means. This isn't fair. I had expected that the experience of oneness would come while in meditation with a candle glowing and incense burning. Or, at least during some moment of incredible sexual orgasm. But in Belfast? In the middle of the street, drowning in fear and rage? Yes. It was perfect that I learn about oneness from the darkness.

Somehow, conversations that I have had with Viet Nam combat veterans come to mind and reinforce that Yes.

Something has shifted for me since that moment. What feels like a cellular learning occurred there and it hasn't all bubbled up to my biocomputer yet, but it has to do with what Oneness really is. What I now know is that oneness is not "nice." It's also not "not-nice." That totality of connection involves both the Light and the Dark, both faces of God. It embraces all of the love, light, goodness, hate, fear and pain that make up our collective experiences of humanness. If we are not open to embracing it all, then the Universe is stuck and unbalanced and, someone or something has to bear the burden of this imbalance. If we learn to resolve the darkness and the light within ourselves, we can, as individuals and collectively, stop projecting our confusion and fear onto others.

Again, we find that the battlefields of the Warrior of the Heart are all *internal*. Again, we remember the Tibetan Buddhist definition, "A Warrior is one who will face his or her own fear." From the Buddhist tradition, "A Warrior is one who has the courage to *know* oneself," to know *all* of yourself, not just the young Belfast mother and baby inside of you, but that British officer inside of you too.

I tell you truthfully that there is a Mahatma Gandhi and a Mother Teresa living in you and in me, waiting to be set free. And, there is also an Adolph Hitler and a Jim Jones in there, who are trying to get out and run things. If you can only own the Light in you and deny the Dark in you, then the Dark will come to rule you. Because you are unwilling to deal with your own Shadow, you will project it out onto others and call them "bad" or "evil," the "enemy." The world is not in the dilemma it is in because of "the bad guys." It's in this mess because of all these "good guys" running around projecting their un-owned darkness onto others and then feeling justified in "fixing" them. Or, if that doesn't work, killing them in the name of God or progress or democracy or even peace!

Meanwhile, Back in Belfast, It's Monday Morning...

...and it's time to reconvene the meeting with the two paramilitary groups.

The meeting gets started a bit late, as things usually do

in Ireland (one Irish definition of "on time" is if you show up before it's over). It isn't very far into the morning before I realize that something is very different today. The two main representatives of the groups are talking *to each other. In fact they are screaming at each other at times, but at least they're interacting. That deadness of Friday and Saturday is gone and in its place is energy, aliveness, communication. What changed? What in the world did these folks do on Sunday to make them begin to open up?*

Then I remembered what I *did on Sunday and things started to get clearer. I had learned something on Sunday that was allowing me to* not *do something on Monday.*

I began to realize that on Thursday, Friday and Saturday, whenever the leaders of these two groups would start to confront one another, I would get scared and I would make some terribly clever intervention. It would have the effect of putting a barrier between them and the confrontation would cease and, of course, so would the communication! Their *way of communicating was to yell and threaten each other and* I *was the one who was feeling threatened so I would use my skill to separate them. My "expert" suggestions or comments were shutting down their contact because I was afraid of the conflict.*

Somehow, something had happened for me out there on the back streets of Belfast on Sunday that had the effect of teaching me one of the most valuable and most simple rules of conflict resolution. It is a rule that I never learned in all my years at three universities and yet it is the most basic rule of all:

YOU CAN'T HAVE CONFLICT *RESOLUTION WITHOUT* CONFLICT.

Of course! Our culture teaches us that conflict is *not* okay. So we try to avoid it, to pretend it doesn't exist, to define peace in terms of zero conflict. Wrong. Conflict *is* okay. In fact, it just IS. If you're a human being, a *live* one, you *will* experience conflict in your life. It's like breathing; it comes with living. But if you're always busy trying to avoid it, you can never resolve it.

Later on, in "Politics of the Heart," I'll talk about my feelings about "peace," and how we can't have peace, *real* peace, without also having conflict. I know that sounds strange, but it just may open the door to a new way of thinking about how to be peaceful.

The Monster Dream

There's a wonderful teaching story about the woman who was having a nightmare. In this nightmare, she was being pursued by a terrible, loathsome monster. For what seemed like hours she tried to get away from it. She ran and ran and hid but the monster always found her. She would escape and run further and further but always this foul-smelling, despicable monster was right behind her, almost close enough to claw her. She ran across meadows and plains, hills and deserts, until finally she could run no more. She had run into a box canyon and the cliff walls were hundreds of feet high all around her. She was trapped. She could feel the hot breath of the monster on her back and, in desperation, she flung herself around, faced the monster and said, "Wha... Wha... What are you going to *do* with me?" The fearsome monster looked down at her and said, "Hell, lady, I don't know. This is *your* dream."

That's right. It's *your* dream. What do you want the monsters in your world to do? Do they have to be really bad so you can be really good? Do they have to be the epitome of darkness so you don't have to deal with your own darkness? It seems that the path of the Heart Warrior asks us to go inward to address these questions, to turn around and face the monsters we have drawn to us "out there," so we can recognize them for who they really are. As long as we continue to run away from our conflicts, they will remain scary monsters who will follow us wherever we go. That which we *resist, persists*.

Coming Home

That Belfast story doesn't end for me in Belfast. That "Monday morning" in Belfast was an important one for the rest of my life. When I had the flash that "you can't have conflict resolution without conflict," somehow it allowed me to get out of the way and let them communicate, even though the communication was bordering on violent. It allowed me to shut up for just a few more minutes before I would say something. It let the "juice" be squeezed a little more, the energy develop more, the "ki" flow and *then*, then we had something to work with. It wasn't "safe" in that room, but it wasn't dead either. You can work with unsafe and alive; you can't work with dead. It reminds me of how Abe Kaplan worked with our group of managers in Ojai, California.

So, here's another teaching that has come to me out of that afternoon on the back streets of Belfast:

Peace, *real* peace, isn't "safe."

(Unless it's the *new*, alive, passionate definition of safe given on page 20)

We got through that Monday in Belfast pretty well. Some minor agreements were reached and most importantly, the two sides got to hear and feel each other in a way they had not before. Usually the meetings between these groups happen through gun sights, and exchanges happen with fire bombs, not words.

So I packed up and headed home. At that time, I was living in an old cabin on a creek in Monte Rio, California. Of course when I got home I had a lot of laundry to do, and seeing as how I had no washing machine, I headed off to the nearest laundromat in Guerneville, about ten miles away. Now, the Guerneville laundromat was the armpit of all laundromats and half the machines were always broken and the working ones were in constant use. You can see what's coming, right?

I walk into the laundromat and, of course, there are no washing machines available. So I wait. I've got a meeting in an hour and I'm worried that I'll be late for it but, no sweat, I'm going to be calm about this and wait peacefully. Well, finally one washing machine becomes available and I rush over to it and cram my three loads of laundry into the one machine, guaranteeing that nothing will get really clean.

When the clothes are done, I dig them out and carry them over to the dryer section in a big lump (there's never any baskets or carts there) and guess what? Right. Half the dryers are broken and the other ones are all in use. I can feel my jaw start to get tight and my breathing get shallow. But, hey, I've had my training in stress management, I've been rolfed and re-birthed and gestalted, I can deal with this. Me upset? Nonsense, I'm too evolved for that. Right.

So, I go back over to a broken washing machine and sit on it, patiently and peacefully waiting for a dryer to become available. A dryer finishes its cycle but no one comes to get their laundry out of it. Another finishes, and another, and still nobody comes and there's no clean surfaces for me to unload their laundry onto. I can feel my tension and anger rising in me as I realize that I'll be late for that meeting. "Why aren't these people more responsible," I mumble as my jaw gets tighter.

But, hey, I'm a peace professional, right? Am I going to let this situation cause me to be un-peaceful? Why, I'll just breathe through it, no sweat. So, I wait and I wait.

Finally, someone comes and removes her laundry from a dryer. I jump down off the washing machine and carry my damp laundry towards this one available dryer, dropping and picking up socks along the way. Just as I get within three feet of the dryer, a woman comes barging in the front door of the laundromat with an armload of soggy, wet clothes. She runs over and cuts right in front of me and throws her clothes into my dryer. Did you get that, that's my dryer. That's the Danaan Parry Memorial Dryer and she stole it.

Immediately, all my training in conflict resolution goes right out the window and I know how I'm going to resolve this - I'm going to push her into the dryer, put a quarter in the slot and watch her go around a few times.

But, I'm a peacemaker, right? So I don't do that, I just go back and sit on the broken washing machine again and try to breathe through it. By now my jaw is really tight but I'm congratulating myself on how peaceful I am and how I've succeeded in not dumping my garbage on other people. Just about the time that I'm feeling really smug about it, I begin to hear a little voice in my head. It says, "Danaan, you're doing the '70's!" What? Speak more clearly, little voice. Again, it says, "Danaan, this is the '80's and you're doing the '70's!" Now, I've come to know my little inner voice never tells me anything but the absolute truth. It may tell me some weird stuff but it always turns out to be totally right-on. Again, it says, "Danaan, get the hell off your washing machine and stop doing the '70's."

Finally, I get it. Finally, I figure out what my inner voice means by "the '70's." It is all of that centering and breathing and calming myself that I've been doing so I wouldn't dump my anger on that woman. Sure, I learned all that in the '70's and it's great stuff, but the present state of our planet now calls upon us to do more than just sit on our washing machines, feeling smug about how peaceful we are. The '90's are calling on us to take the next step, to get off our washing machines and our meditation benches and our ivory towers and relate to one another as real human beings.

Okay, so off my washing machine I get! I put my laundry on top of the machine and I go over and sit down next to the woman who "stole my dryer." I can hear my heart beating like a drum inside my chest; this is my Belfast! "Hi, there," I say to her and she looks at me like I'm some creep on the make. "I need to talk to you about what just happened," I say, "I'm feeling pretty strongly about how you cut in front of me and took that dryer." On and on I go, giving her my whole "movie," all four reels of it, about how I had waited patiently and about how late I was for my meeting, etc., etc.... She listened. Then, it was her turn and, boy, did I get her whole movie! Guess what? I wasn't in her movie; I didn't even have a bit part in it. In her movie, I didn't "steal her dryer," she didn't even see me. In her movie, I got to hear about her broken dryer at home, about her three kids who were out in her car, demolishing the upholstery and about a husband who was due home in a half hour and who wanted his dinner on time. As we sat and shared for about ten minutes, we began to get some glimpse of two different realities touching one another.

And, that's it! That's the end of the story. No flashy ending, no walking off arm-in-arm into the sunset. No, she did not take her laundry out of the dryer for me, and no, we did not develop a "significant relationship." But, for a few minutes, there was a space created for two people to talk and to listen to one another and I left that small encounter feeling clean and whole and peaceful. I left that brief "peace conference" with the awareness that this is how world peace is made, not in diplomatic summit meetings or in massive rallies but in the laundromats and offices and bedrooms of our daily lives. You and I, ordinary people in ordinary situations, are "getting off our washing machines" (letting go of our positions), and choosing to risk rejection and attack to create peace in the only place where it can be created - in the intimacy of personal contact. Such is the courage of the Warrior of the Heart.

Exercise

GET OFF YOUR WASHING MACHINE!

One of the things that I tell the people who take my Warrior of the Heart Training is that "there's a Laundromat out there somewhere with your name on it!"

What I mean is that we all are given those moments wherein we are called to move beyond our old ways of reacting to a situation and practice new, more growth producing behaviors.

So my questions to you are: Where's *your* laundromat? What washing machine do you need to get your buns off of so that you can go over and sit down next to _____ and say your truth and listen, really listen, to the truth of another?

Let's play with the metaphor a bit and see what you can uncover...

Who "stole" *your* dryer (who has treated you unfairly, has ripped you off, been mean and hurting to you?)?

Their name:

What did they do?

How did you feel?

What did you do about it?

Let's just fantasize that you are now creating a situation wherein you, metaphorically, "get off your washing machine" and go over and sit next to _____ . How would you do that? What would it look like? How could you help to make it a "safe space?"

What new outcome would you like to see happen?

In this new outcome, did you

a) remember and communicate that *your* truth is just the way you saw it, not necessarily THE truth?

b) assure your partner that he/she will have equal time wherein you will really listen, so please listen to me now?

c) remember that the "presenting" problem is rarely the real problem and that conflict is usually a cry for intimacy?

d) commit yourself to being 100% present which requires you to suspend your "position" for a while? (your position can be seen above in your answer to "what did they do?")

It may be time for you to find a way to set up a meeting with this person and try your new skills at Conflict Resolution. If you and she/he just can relax and listen to the other without trying to fix it, it might loosen something up. It might point to a whole new way of seeing the problem and each other that was impossible to see before. This is referred to later in the book as "living in-between the trapezes" (see page 81.)

3
WAYS OF BEING

Chapter 9

Centering

AIKIDO AND THE WARRIOR

There can be no finer symbolic representation of the Way of the Peaceful Warrior than the graceful yet powerful Japanese ideograms that describe the soft martial art of Aikido.

AI 合

KI 氣

DO 道

The first ideogram is Ai or Harmony. The second is Ki (or Chi in Chinese) as in Tai Chi Chuan. It means energy, pure energy, universal life force, the flowing electric field between us. In the popular movie *Star Wars*, when the teacher Obiewan Kenobe says to the young Luke Skywalker, "May the Force be with you," he is speaking of Ki. Finally, there is Do or Tao (pronounced DOW) which means "the way, the path."

Then, AiKiDo means "the *way* of *harmonizing* with the *life force*, the path of blending with pure energy." The significance of this to the Warrior of the Heart becomes clear when we notice that most people spend their lives acting as if they had only some small, easily depletable, personal source of energy. It's as if they thought that the only energy they had available to them came from a few cheap D-cell batteries in their little inner battery pack. With that belief system, one has to be very careful not to "run down," not to take chances, not to seize life and live it fully. One gets *tired* easily, gets *sick* frequently and just generally needs to guard against anyone who might be a drain on their D-cells.

The Warrior knows better. As a Warrior, you discover that your energy comes from being in harmony with Ki, with the life force. It is all around you, available always in unlimited quantity. No puny battery pack for you; rather an inalienable right to plug into Ki, to swim effortlessly in the river of the universal energy field, sharing that energy with all who flow in this river.

We must come to know Ki as we know a dear friend so that it will be available for us when and where we need it on our Warrior path. Perhaps the best way to develop this sense of Ki is to study the soft art of Aikido itself. Aikido is the martial art with no offensive moves; you couldn't *start* a fight with it if you wanted to. But you certainly can work with the energy if someone else starts a fight. Aikido is a wonderful medium for learning how to transform negative energy into positive energy so that it may be returned with love. Learning Aikido would be a perfect adjunct to the path we shall follow in this book, and I encourage you to consider taking a dozen classes given by a reputable sensei (teacher) in a professional dojo (training studio) in your area. (Tai Chi Chuan, the moving meditation, is another useful art.)

It is now important that you begin to develop a sense of Ki. It's not *your* Ki or anybody's Ki; it just *is*. If you try to hold onto it or possess it (or anything else), it will become stagnant and sour and affect your life negatively.

If you embrace Ki and allow it to flow through you like a river, it will fill you and empower you. The more Ki you allow to flow through you, the more you will have available in your life.

I'm sure that by now you are aware that you can replace the word Ki with just about *any* word that represents something you want more of in your life. The more _____ , love, money, caring, acknowledgement, etc. you let flow through you to others, the more of it you will have available in your own life. It's sadly interesting to me that our society is set up to teach us to hold on, to possess and accumulate. "Hoard that money; don't spread your love around; don't relate to strangers; get it while the gettin's good." Those are exactly the rules for creating *lack* in your life. I guess this is a culture addicted to lack! Are you?

Finding Your Power Center

There is a place in your physical body that is referred to as "the reservoir of Ki," the Hara in Japanese, the *power center*. It is at the physical center of your weight-mass and when you hear someone say, "I feel un-centered" or "I need to get in touch with my center," the Hara is the actual physical space in them that they have lost connection with. Ki, the life force, streams into you and through you, pooling, as it were, in your reservoir, your power center. To prevent this reservoir from getting stagnant, the Warrior constantly empties the pool while filling it at the same time.

Let's develop a physical sense of that Hara, that *power center* in you. It is vital that you be in touch with your center so that your actions are "centered." Having a sense of your *center* gives you a feeling of balance, of groundedness, of okayness and inner security that help you to radiate positive power to your world.

Develop a mental image of your Hara, your power center. It is somewhere deep down in your torso, below your navel and in the center of you. (Many people have their center located in their head, their intellect, primarily because they have cut themselves off from the rest of their body. This results in their stumbling their way through life, always feeling uncentered because they have placed their consciousness so far up in their heads.) The Warrior way is to get that center low, low in your torso, so that it is working WITH gravity, helping to keep you grounded, instead of fighting against gravity, always in fear of falling on your face.

An Exercise to Find Your Power Center

Now I ask you to stand up with this book in your hands. Place your feet about shoulder length apart, making sure that your feet are parallel to one another and perpendicular to your body (no pigeon-toes, please). Check that your weight is equally distributed on both feet.

Unlock your knees. Don't bend them too much; simply bend them slightly so that they become shock-absorbers and so that you do not cut off the energy flowing through your knees.

Now, as you read these words, begin a slight, gentle swaying motion to the left and right by switching the weight from one foot to the other. As you sway from side to side, imagine that you are sliding along an imaginary line that runs through your lower hip joints. So, here you are, sliding along this imaginary line, then reversing direction and sliding along it the other way, then the other direction, and again, and again. Rocking from side to side, sliding left and right along this imaginary line. Can you feel it? Keep swaying. Breathe!

In a few moments, when you have read this paragraph, I want you to close your eyes. Just let the book hang in one hand with a finger keeping the place. With your eyes closed, continue to sway and imagine that there is a mark on the line, a mark right at *center*. As you slide along this line, you pass through this center mark, go beyond it, change direction and pass through it again. Over and over, passing through center. Close your eyes and continue swaying until you have developed some sense of this center mark on the line, then come to a slow stop and open your eyes. Okay, *now*, it's time to do it; close your eyes, begin swaying and feel that center mark.

Next Step

Hello. Don't lose the sense of center in you. Keep breathing normally and begin another swaying motion: this time, *forward* and *backward* by simply rocking your pelvis. Your body should be moving gracefully in a direction perpendicular to the previous rocking motion. As before, imagine that you are sliding along an imaginary line that runs through your lower torso, a line that crosses the previous line exactly at *center*. Just keep rocking back and forth, slowly, enjoying the ride and keeping your consciousness right down there in your lower belly as you slide forward and backward along the line.

Next Step

When you have read this paragraph, close your eyes and let the book hang in one hand with the place saved. With your eyes closed, bring *all* your attention to that line, to that crossover point where the left/right line crosses the forward/backward line. Here is your *center*, your reservoir of Ki. Close your eyes and allow your sense of this place in you to deepen and deepen. Take your time and, when you're ready, open your eyes and stand still, in touch with your center. *Now,* close your eyes, sway forward and backward and feel your *center.*

Next Step

Hello, again. Again, retain the sense of CENTER. Connect with your Hara, bring all your awareness to that place. Feel your belly expand as you breathe deeply into it. Take the fingers of your right hand and press them into your lower belly down where your center resides, deep in your torso. Press in with your fingers so that you send a message to your brain, your bio-computer, which says, "Yes, this is where my power center is, deep in my belly, where it helps me to be centered and grounded. It's not up in my head making me unbalanced and fearful of being 'pushed around.' It's low, working with gravity, and all is well."

Keeping your right hand on your lower belly, read this paragraph. Then put the book down, remain standing and bring your left hand up to cover your heart. Place it over your actual heart or your heart center in the middle of your chest, whichever feels more right to you. Acknowledge that the path of the Warrior of the Heart is the path that connects the power center with the heart center. Close your eyes and visualize a channel connecting these two centers. Use your breath to open wide this channel so that the energy of power and the energy of love can flow to one another and combine. As a Warrior of the Heart, you must always be in intimate connection with both your power *and* your love because power without the heart becomes cold and manipulative and corrupt. *And,* love without power leaves the Warrior unable to participate in the positive change process that our planet cries out for. Your path is to hold them both within you. Your task is to use your power with love to love your world powerfully.

Okay. Put the book down, cover your heart with your left hand, keep your right hand on your power center and press firmly into your power center and your heart center. Breathe deeply and OPEN THAT CHANNEL. Three or four minutes of deep breathing should do for now.

What are you feeling this first time? Have you a sense of your Hara and your heart, the centers that the Warrior must keep open and connected as you do your work in the world? I recommend that you do this exercise every time you know that you are about to have a confrontation with someone so that your power will always come through your heart as you share in the intimacy of that conflict with that "dance partner." But now, please write down your feelings about your power and heart centers so that you will be able to come back to this first opening later.

Feelings:

The time has come for us to speak about Power.

Chapter 10

Power

ENERGY MANIFESTED IN TIME

Now Woman Warrior
I Move Out And Into Life
Yin And Yang Balanced
                    Maryann

We must learn to reclaim our own internal power for good. It is not powerful people who rob others of their rights. It is those who feel powerless inside who must oppress. When you and I and enough of us own our ability to affect positive change in our lives, on our planet, only then will we begin to create the age of evolutionary consciousness that we talk so much about.
                    Danaan

POWER

What a powerful word! The mere mention of the word usually scares the pants off of people. The concept of Power is so intimately related to the Warrior path that we must go beyond its boogey-man facade and seek to understand power for what it truly is.

"When the power of love overcomes the love of power, then there will be true peace."
                    Sri Chin Moi Gosh

I'm sure that you are familiar with the phrase "Power corrupts; absolute power corrupts absolutely." If this is true, how can you as a Warrior of the Heart aspire to the conscious ownership of your full range of power? Yet this is exactly what must occur for you to know yourself and to be effective in the world. The answer is that "power," in itself, is neither good nor bad. Power does not corrupt. "Power" in its essential state has no value judgment associated with it, just as "behavior" has no positive or negative connotation until someone *does* something with it. **Power is simply energy manifested in time.** What the individual chooses to do with that manifestation of energy is what determines its positive or negative inclination. Throughout history the primary inclination has been to use power in a negative fashion, rather than positive, because it is a matter of where the power comes from, the "locus of power."

It would be a worthwhile venture for one embarking on today's Warrior path to study the figures in history that utilized large amounts of power. A study not of "what they did" but of "who they were" will clarify the concept of power and its positive and negative use. There are only two types of world leaders that have successfully wielded power. One type is personified by arch-villains such as Hitler, Mussolini, Nero and Herod. The other type, at an extreme in behavior style, is personified by passionately loved heroes such as Jesus, Gandhi, Buddha, Mother Theresa, Dag Hammerskjold and Martin Luther King. It's fascinating to uncover the very simple common-denominator present in each type and also the simple difference between the types. It's not complicated at all. It's just a matter of *where* their power comes from.

In the case of the arch-villains, a look at their early childhood clearly shows that they came from a position of utter power-lessness. For them, their center of power was somewhere *external* to their being. Power was something out there that had to be seized and manipulated. Lacking a sense of internal power, they grabbed on to external power and misused it to its extreme.

A look at the lives of the folk heroes shows men and women who felt their power from *within*. The source of their tremendous power lay inside their being, not outside where it must be achieved. When they used their power in the world, there was never any fear that it could be stolen from them or used up or worn out. Their source of power was as a wellspring deep within their Self, never faltering, never decreasing in its flow. Power and love were one for them and the more they gave of these, the more there was to give.

It is so with the Heart Warrior. Power does not corrupt. Those who cannot sense their internal wellspring of power and love are the ones who *choose* to corrupt with the power that they have stolen from outside themselves.

The Warrior knows that his or her internal wellspring of power and love is constantly re-nourished by self-power and self-love. The Warrior's sense of self can never be taken away.

The Warrior walks the path of power as did the high beings of pure love and pure power who are known to us now as Jesus, Gandhi, Buddha, Krishna and White Eagle. If you wish to deepen your knowledge not only of power, but of total love and yielding (the art of giving up "position" to make a space for everyone to win), then there can be no finer place to begin than with the lives of these beings.

On your own personal journey, you will encounter moments wherein you will know your source of power. It may occur in the midst of deep meditation. It may overtake you as you immerse yourself in a moment of intensity. It may fill you as you consciously yield in the face of aggressive challenge. Or, it may simply come unannounced and uninvited in the mundane "getting on with life." But you will know briefly, that you are different, unique. You are. In a flash, you will understand that you have everything you could ever need to be whatever you wish to be. You will know that a Source flows within you that will never cease.

This awareness occurs to *all* conscious beings, everywhere. *But,* almost everyone chooses instantaneously to disregard this moment, to discount it. When we have been trained from childhood to fear and mistrust our own power, it's understandable that we would try to deny it when it bubbles up. But, if you choose the path of the Warrior, you must learn to cherish this gift and to utilize your power in the service of love. Your Will, — your conscious Will, will make the difference between the correct and incorrect use of your power.

> "I realize suddenly that it is not a question of faith,
> but of will. I WILL life to go on. We have collectively
> created the death cults. We can collectively create a
> culture of life.But to do so, we must be willing to step
> out of line, to forego the comfort of leaving decisions
> up to somebody else. To will is to make our own
> decisions, guide our own lives, commit ourselves, our
> time, our work, our energy, to act in the service of life.
> To will is to reclaim our power, our power to reclaim
> the future."
>
> *Starhawk, The Spiral Dance*

As a Warrior of the Heart, you understand that your power is a dreadful thing; dreadful in its true sense. The archaic form of "dreadful" means "inspiring awe or reverence; an awesome reverence inspired by something sacred."

Since we each create our reality, participate in the creation of group concensus reality and since the use of your Warrior power is a dreadful force in this creation, it is your responsibility to remain conscious in your actions.

The development of your Warrior proceeds along many parallel paths as your Will becomes more and more focused.

There will come a moment when you will notice that you are capable of choosing when and where to manifest your internal power in external situations so as to change the flow of that situation. This is the moment when conscious responsibility for who you are becomes of paramount importance.

Exercise

Please identify who your heroes are. Think about the people who inspire you; those who represent for you the highest ideals to which you aspire.

Hero #1_____

Write down some of the qualities this person has:

1.   2.

3.   4.

5.   6.

Hero #2_____

Write down some of his/her qualities:

1.   2.

3.   4.

5.   6.

Hero #3_____

Write down some of his/her qualities:

1.   2.

3.   4.

5.   6.

Please underline those qualities that you experience in *yourself* as well.

Now list a few of those people who are arch-villains in your judgment; those who represent the evil and degradation in the world.

Villain #1_____

Write down some of the characteristics of this person:

1.   2.

3.

Villain #2_____

Write down some of the characteristics of this person:

1.   2.

3.

Villain #3_____

Write down some of the characteristics of this person:

1.   2.

3.

Take a good look at the "negative" qualities that you have assigned to your "bad guys." It just may be that you can learn something about what is in your own "shadow" from these words. We tend to recognize and count as important those negative characteristics in others which we have stuffed down into our own shadows and try to ignore in ourselves. Go back and look at the "Persona-Shadow-Self" sphere you filled out for yourself on page 37 and see if anything needs to be added there in light of the lists you have made here.

Chapter 11

Yielding

THE CONCEPT OF SOFT POWER

The Brook Talks To Me
Ever Flowing Gentleness
Yet So Powerful

Charles

Soft Power

To understand what real power is, let me tell you a story about a modern day Aikido Master and the use of *soft* power.

About 15 years ago, I was searching for a physical discipline that would be complementary with my spiritual growth. I checked out Karate, Tai Quon Do, Judo and others and they all felt too aggressive and too ego-centered to me (that doesn't mean that they actually are but simply that it was my experience of those I checked out this way). Then I encountered a man who was the foremost American Aikido master, having attained every honor and title that Aikido had to give. His clarity and centeredness immediately drew me in, not to mention his delightful sense of humor. But above all, his incredible compassion and loving respect for all about him was evident in every gesture. He told me a story I will never forget.

It happened after 25 years of studying Aikido and after 15 years of teaching Aikido. Suddenly, after training thousands of students, he began to wonder... "does this stuff really work?" All of his experience had been in the dojo, all of his partners (Aikido never recognizes the idea of opponent, only partners) had been teachers, colleagues and students. What about out there, on the street, would Aikido really work?

Well, of course, as soon as he began to question, the universe provided him with a way to check it out. (Whoever is running this universe has a perverse sense of cosmic humor, I've noticed). Shortly thereafter, he was in Honolulu at an Aikido competition. He took all the top honors and decided to celebrate. He and his buddies went to a bar and had a few. And a few more. Suddenly, it was closing time and they were pretty loaded as the bartender shoved them out the door. As they staggered down the streets of Honolulu, one by one his friends said good night and went into their hotels. Finally, he was all alone, looking for his hotel and realizing that he was completely lost. He didn't know where he was but he did know he was not in a wonderful part of town. The street got narrower and turned into an alley. From the far end of the alley around the corner came five, yes five, very big and very drunk Samoans. When they saw him they began yelling obscenities, threatening him and, as they moved towards him, telling him exactly what they were going to do with the small pieces of his body that would be left after they were through with him.

His first thought was, "Thanks a lot, God! Guess I'm about to get what I asked for, whether I want it or not." His next thought was, "Okay, for my fifth degree black belt, I had to deal with five partners. Guess I'll have to do it again out here in the real world," and he began his breathing, his centering, his extending of Ki.

Then, something happened. As the five men got to within about twenty feet of him, he suddenly remembered what Ai-Ki-Do is really all about and why he never had to check it out on the streets. With this awareness, he performed the only truly appropriate Aikido move for that situation — he turned around and ran like hell!

I said to myself, "This man is my teacher." This man knows something I do not know. I realized that, at the level of awareness I was at, I would have not been able to "run away." I would have had to stay there and *prove* something. I would have been unable to let go of my *position* and therefore I would have been part of the problem, not part of the solution. What he realized in those last few moments was that for him to stand there would have created a classic win/lose battle. Either he would have won and they would have lost or vice-versa. In either case, everyone would have lost. If *anyone* loses, everyone loses. If you don't believe that, take a look at all the win/lose wars that have been fought down through the centuries. Who won? Take a look at your own wars, the ones you fight with family, friends, bosses, neighbors, shopkeepers. If one of you loses, does the other really win? What occurs is a back-and-forth seesaw struggle for victory in the *next* battle. The one who loses first gets smarter next time. To break out of the seesaw game of serial battlegrounds, you must yield your position so that the possibility of win/win solutions can be discovered.

The Aikido teacher was a bit drunk. He was lost and disoriented, uncentered, in a place where he shouldn't be. To engage would only create winners and losers. He chose the only non-lose/lose alternative, he got out of there. In the process, he remembered (re-member) why he had never encountered this negative energy before. It was because he hadn't *needed* to.

In Aikido, it is said that a true Sensei uses Ki to transform conflict at the level of pure energy. If the situation becomes such that the Sensei has to use physical force to deal with the conflict, then obviously the Sensei has been asleep. It would be a disgrace for a true Sensei to allow the conflict to get to the more dense physical level before he or she resolved it. This, then, is the power of Ki. This is an example of the art of *Yielding*.

Chapter 12

Position

"A WARRIOR NEEDS NO PLACE TO STAND"
— Buddhist tradition

My Heart Is The Light
Sharing With My Darkest Side
Knowing It's Okay
Charles

In the martial art of Aikido, one learns that holding on to one's position causes one to lose. Because if anyone loses, everyone loses, it is necessary to participate in action wherein everyone wins. This requires letting go of your *position*.

Positions are usually ways of seeing things, judgments about "how it is" or how it should be. Positions involve the need to be "right." They signal that our center of power is outside us, rather than inside, that our sense of okay-ness comes from others, not from our calm center.

In a number of ancient traditions, it is said that "a warrior has and needs no place to stand." No *position*. No attachments.

The attitude of the Warrior of the Heart is best described by what I call the Parable of the Trapeze. It clearly describes the places where the Warrior belongs:

The Parable of the Trapeze

Turning the fear of transformation into the transformation of fear.

Sometimes I feel that my life is a series of trapeze swings. I'm either hanging on to a trapeze bar swinging along or, for a few moments in my life, I'm hurtling across space in between trapeze bars.

Most of the time, I spend my life hanging on for dear life

to my trapeze-bar-of-the-moment. It carries me along at a
certain steady rate of swing and I have the feeling that I'm
in control of my life. I know most of the right questions and
even some of the answers.

But, every once in a while as I'm merrily (or even not-
so-merrily) swinging along, I look out ahead of me into the
distance and what do I see? I see another trapeze bar
swinging toward me. It's empty and I know, in that place
in me that knows, that this new trapeze bar has my name
on it. It is my next step, my growth, my aliveness coming
to get me. In my heart-of-hearts I know that, for me to grow,
I must release my grip on this present, well-known bar and
move to the new one.

Each time it happens to me I hope (no, I pray) that I
won't have to let go of my old bar completely before I grab
the new one. But in my knowing place, I know that I must
totally release my grasp on my old bar and, for some
moment in time, I must hurtle across space before I can
grab onto the new bar.

Each time, I am filled with terror. It doesn't matter that
in all my previous hurtles across the void of unknowing I
have always made it. I am each time afraid that I will miss,
that I will be crushed on unseen rocks in the bottomless
chasm between bars. I do it anyway. Perhaps this is the
essence of what the mystics call the faith experience. No
guarantees, no net, no insurance policy, but you do it
anyway because somehow to keep hanging on to that old
bar is no longer on the list of alternatives. So, for an
eternity that can last a microsecond or a thousand life-
times, I soar across the dark void of "the past is gone, the
future is not yet here." It's called "transition". I have come
to believe that this transition is the only place that real
change occurs. I mean real change, not the pseudo-
change that only lasts until the next time my old buttons
get punched.

I have noticed that, in our culture, this transition zone
is looked upon as a "no-thing," a no-place between
places. Sure, the old trapeze bar was real and, that new
one coming towards me, I hope that's real, too. But the
void in between? Is that just a scary, confusing, disorient-
ing nowhere that must be gotten through as fast and as

*unconsciously as possible? NO! What a wasted opportu-
nity that would be. I have a sneaking suspicion that the
transition zone is the only real thing and the bars are
illusions we dream up to avoid the void where the real
change, the real growth occurs for us. Whether or not my
hunch is true, it remains that the transition zones in our
lives are incredibly rich places. They should be honored,
even savored. Yes, with all the pain and fear and feelings
of being out of control that can (but not necessarily)
accompany transitions, they are still the most alive, most
growth-filled, passionate, expansive moments in our lives.*

> **"We cannot discover new oceans unless we have
> the courage to lose sight of the shore."**
> **Anonymous**

So, transformation of fear may have nothing to do with
making fear go away but rather with giving ourselves permission to "hang-out" in the transition between trapezes. Transforming our need to grab that new bar, any bar, is allowing
ourselves to dwell in the only place where change really
happens. It can be terrifying. It can also be enlightening in the
true sense of the word. Hurtling through the void, we just may
learn how to fly.

If the Warrior of the Heart can be described with one term,
then that term is *changemaker*. Since the only place that
change can really happen is out there, in between trapezes,
then this is the place where the Heart Warrior belongs.

> **"The Warrior has and needs no place to stand,
> no position to cling to."**
> *Unknown*

> **"The means is the end in the process of becoming."**
> *Jacques Maritain*

Exercise

Let's spend a little time using this "Trapeze" image to identify some areas of "stuckness" and potential movement in our lives. The following is a simple way for you to outline where you feel that you are "holding on" and to explore how you might "let go" of that old trapeze, to evoke some forward movement towards a more alive, passionate you. Don't analyze this too much. Just write down that which wants to come out.

What are the places of growth, of life-affirming positive change that are calling to me in areas A, B and C?

A. In my own personal inner life (me in relationship with me):

Hanging on
Ways of being that are not helping me to fly (the old trap)

Letting go
The Process (the "letting go" that needs to happen)

Tomorrow's trapeze
This is who my heart tells me I can be

Here is one concrete step that I *will* accomplish in the next three months:

B. In my love relationships (me in relationship to the one or ones I most dearly love):

Hanging on
Unfulfilling ways I act in relationship

Letting go
The Process

Tomorrow's trapeze
A new win/win way of being in relationship

Here is one concrete step that I <u>will</u> accomplish in the next three months:

C. In my relationship to my planet (me, the earth, our shared planetary predicament and my global family):

Hanging on
Attitudes and behaviors that no longer lead to harmony, security and abundance for our global family

Letting go
The Process of Change

Tomorrow's trapeze
Ways of being that will create a world that works

> **Here is one concrete step that I <u>will</u> accomplish in the next three months:**

Chapter 13

Integrity

FOLLOWING YOUR INNER TRUTH

I Came Not Knowing
But I Found The Warrior
In Integrity

　　　　　　　Pete

A friend of mine, one of the best Aikidoists I know, was in Tokyo for a gathering of Aikido teachers. After it was over, he wanted to visit his teacher in Kyoto in the south of Japan.

It was there that he found himself standing on one of those high speed Japanese trains where they pack you in like sardines. As they hurtled down the track, he became aware that he was the only Caucasian on the train. He also heard a loud commotion going on at the opposite end of the train car. The train was so packed with people that it took him a while to figure out what was going on but, as the train lurched from side to side, he could see past people's heads that a very large and very drunken Japanese man was yelling and pushing people, cursing and grabbing food from those around him and just being a general pain in the you-know-what.

After watching this scene unfold for awhile, my friend began to think almost unconsciously, "That guy is lucky I'm not at his end of this car; I'd teach him some manners."

Well, the minute he formulated that thought, the big drunk at the opposite end of the car stopped what he was doing. My friend said that the drunk began searching the train car with his eyes until finally he was staring directly at my friend. At this moment, my friend whispered to himself, "Oh, shit." He had extended his Ki to this man and the man had accepted his offer to "dance." Before my friend had barely figured out what was happening, the drunk was screaming at him, "Get off our train, you white devil; you killed all my people," and he began to claw his way through the packed aisle to get at my friend.

"What to do?" my friend thought. "All the doors are locked; I can barely raise my arms. I guess if he gets to me, I'll put him on the floor as quickly as possible and then, at the next station, I'll show him the wisdom of taking the next train." My friend grounded and centered himself, began his deep breathing and waited for the drunk to come to him.

But, as this big drunk squeezed past people to get to my friend, he happened to pass a seat where a very old, thin Japanese man was sitting. As he passed, the old man reached up and placed his hand on the big man's shoulder. The startled drunk threw down the old man's hand with a threat but the old man immediately put it back. Again, the drunk threw the hand off his shoulder, promising to break the hand if he didn't mind his own business. But again, gently, the hand returned to the shoulder.

My friend said that this dance must have gone on for eight or nine more rounds. Hand up on the drunk's shoulder, thrown off, back up, off, up, like some primal mating ritual of the Blue Heron. After the eighth or ninth cycle the old man, for the first time, looked up at the drunk, made eye contact and said softly, "So, you drink on trains, eh?" The drunk again threw down the hand, the old man immediately replaced it and said, "I drink on trains, too. All my family are dead. I'm old and all alone. When I'm in a crowd of people, like on this train, I get so lonely, I drink to forget." Now, the drunk was listening. The old man continued, "Are you lonely, too, my young brother?"

About one minute later, the big man was sitting on the arm of the old man's seat with his head resting on the old man's shoulder. The old man was stroking his matted hair as the big man sobbed uncontrollably, "I'm so lonely; I hurt so much. Nobody loves me. I'm so alone."

And there's my friend, still in his Aikido position, feeling like a fool.

If ever there were a model for Aikido, for transformation of seemingly negative energy into positive, peace-filled possibility, here it was. That old man perhaps never even heard of

Aikido but, nonetheless, he was an Aikido master par excellence. The reason I tell you this story now is because the old man is a perfect example of soft power and the embodiment of a quality that you and I must always strive for in our work of positive change-making. That quality is *Integrity*.
You see, that old Japanese man was not lying. He really *did* drink on trains. He wasn't making up some clever story to hook that big guy. He really was lonely and so he could reach out with integrity to his brother-in-pain. From his own woundedness, he could authentically connect with the woundedness of another.

> "He who attempts to act and think for others or for the world without deepening his own self-understanding, freedom, integrity and capacity to love, will not have anything to give others. He will communicate to them nothing but the contagion of his own obsessions, his aggressiveness, his ego-centered ambitions, his delusions about ends and means, his doctrinaire prejudices and ideas."
>
> **Thomas Merton**

How often we "helpers" are tempted to "manufacture" therapeutic interventions to rescue someone. But that's just the old persecutor/victim/ rescuer triangle. The *rescuer* actually is part of the problem not the solution. All three are necessary parts of the triangle and we usually find that the three positions "change roles" so that today's rescuer is tomorrow's oppressor, etc.

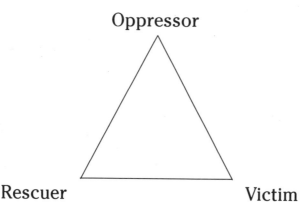

Oppressor

Rescuer   Victim

Authentic transformation of energy comes from Integrity. Integrity means that you come from a place of inner truth to relate to a similar place of truth in another. Because the concept of creating positive change holds great power, it demands of us a deep sense of integrity. This integrity is called for in the *means*, the process we use, just as much as the *ends*, the goal we aspire to. The end *never* justifies the means if the means are not infused with integrity. *How* we create peace is just as important as it's creation.

As I write this, I'm reminded of my time with Mother Teresa and the new definition of Service that I learned while with her. I'm also reminded of my "signature-gathering" experience for the nuclear freeze, which has to do with Integrity. When we talk about Power, we must always remember: Power and Integrity *must* go hand-in-hand.

Mother Teresa: A new model of service

"It's not how much we do but how much love we put in the action that we do."

**Mother Teresa, in her
Nobel Prize speech**

In 1978, I found myself stranded in Bombay, India and through an interesting array of non-coincidences, I was taken in and fed by the Catholic Bishop of Bombay. On the day I was to fly out of India, the Bishop called for his limousine and off we drove through the steaming streets toward the airport.

On the way, he mentioned that Mother Teresa was in town, setting up a hospice on the docks. She had kicked the Indian government out of two warehouses left over from the British East India Company and was moving in hundreds of old men and women. As I'm sure you know, she and her supporters drive around in pickup trucks and bring back the cast-offs of Indian society who are drowning in their own urine in the gutters of Calcutta, Bombay, etc. She heals them with soup and with love and respect.

The Bishop casually asked if I would like to meet Mother Teresa. WOULD I? You bet!

The next thing I knew, we were standing in front of those warehouses and he was pushing me towards the door. From then on, it got a little hazy. I walked into love. Many days later, I staggered out of there, having missed my plane, expired my visa and it didn't matter. I had been filled.

For once in my life, I had known total peace. I had scrubbed the knees of dying old men, changed sheets for a hundred twisted bodies, mopped up rivers of urine and it was, in every second, exactly what I wanted to do. There was not one moment in which I questioned my motives or my effectiveness or my salary. Not once did I worry about working too hard or if I was being taken advantage of or underaffirmed. I worked all night and was filled with energy.

One day, a little Indian nun came up to me and said, "Mr. Parry, you must go home." Anxiety attack! "I must have done it wrong," my ego cried. She said, "This is not your place. You have come here to learn about fullness. You have learned it. Now go home and find it in your place."

Fullness. Loving doing what you do. Doing what you love to do. It's the most important thing in the world.

For most of us, life consists of working at jobs that do NOT fill us up, but rather drain our lust for life. We do this so that we can make the money that will allow us to afford the experiences and materials that will make us happy. It doesn't work. Happiness, fullness, even abundance are not entities in themselves. They are by-products. We achieve these treasures not directly but when we have found our right place in the unfolding of it all. The secret is to identify that which fills you up when you do it and then do it with all your heart. Do it as if it were your gift to the world, your pearl of great price. Make it the most perfect gift that you can ever give and give it fully.

The point is this — if you cannot give yourself to your work, then not only will it not nourish you, it will impoverish everyone. It is not the external product that matters, it is the quality of the energy that made it that matters. We seem to attach so much importance to the outcome of our labor, to the goal, to the product; we many times ignore the process by which we arrive at that outcome or by which we achieve that goal.

Let me tell you a little story about the time I was collecting signatures for the Nuclear Freeze amendment.

I was in a shopping center and when anyone passed, I would ask them to sign the petition. When one particularly harried woman, laden with boxes and bags, was asked, she said, "I don't have time." I pressed her a little harder and finally she took my pen and scribbled her name on the sheet without reading any of what she was signing. She had signed just to get me off her back. Within minutes a young man walked by and I encountered him. My 6'3" highly assertive stance clearly intimidated him and he signed. I think he would have signed a blank check to get me out of his way. Next to come along was a woman and her child. The woman looked at the petition, read it over and said, "What a great idea! Of course I'll sign and thank you for doing this." Off she went, leaving me feeling seen and filled.

As I thought about these three encounters, I became clear about how totally different they had been. I had a fantasy that in each case a zap of energy was released into the universe to be added to the collective energy. In the first encounter, the energy zapped into the universe was full of hassle, loaded with "bother, bother." The second zap was full of intimidation, "don't pick on me." The third was full of love, colored with hues of trust and caring. At one level, I had accomplished my goal in all three. I had three more signatures to turn in and the signature counters would never know the difference. But I would. Those three signers would. In some way, the different types of emotions involved in those encounters were far more important than any number of signatures on any petition.

Since then, I've become pretty clear about the quality, the color of the energy that I want to release into the universe. If I can't collect signatures with love, if I can't accomplish my goals in a way that adds to the reservoir of positive energy in the world, then I better do something wherein I can. But of course the real growth step is not in running off to "something else." It is in transforming myself in the midst of the difficult situation. When I come from a place of love, when my gift to the world is myself, rather than what I produce, then every occasion is an opportunity to add to that positive energy bank.

That's my ideal. I'm not there yet. So, on my way, I sometimes need to move away from situations wherein I cannot give my gift fully because the environment is not conducive to the sharing of that gift. Whatever the choice, some things remain true. The end never justifies the means. The process may be what's important, not the goal. The concept of "working to make money so that we can afford to be happy" is a cruel joke. If you are not enjoying your work, then no amount of money will make you as happy as when you take the risk to do what you love to do. Then you won't have to buy happiness, it will come with the territory. Yes, I know that the transition period between the two types of work is usually difficult, many times confusing. But when you finally click into that which fills you, you are not only nurturing yourself, you are nurturing us all. We really are all connected, you know.

Chapter 14

Presence

THE DOLPHINS

The Waves Of My Life
Wash Upon The Shore And Die
My Ocean Lives On

> DANAAN

"To be 100% present is to make your life work."

Be 100% Present

When I want to *really* relax and nourish myself, I go to the dolphins. For years, dolphins and whales have been my teachers, my source of regeneration. Just to be around them fills me with joy. It's one of the main reasons I choose to live on an island in Puget Sound. A simple ferry boat ride to Seattle or a kayak ride around the point can yield a spectacle of dancing, leaping dolphins or orca whales. In this wild, natural encounter, I am reminded of my own naturalness and my own beauty.

A few years ago, my son Michael and I were in Baja California, that magnificent spit of desert that belongs to Mexico but bears little connection to mainland Mexico. It is its own wild world. We were camped down by the southern tip, slightly up into the Gulf of California, on the rocky beach of a bay that I knew was a favorite hanging-out place for dolphins.

We had a small sunfish sailboat with us. On the second day, we encountered a pod of dolphins, about eight of them. For about half an hour, we played together, the dolphins swimming alongside the boat, rubbing up against it, raising their heads up to the gunwale and looking at us with that big, gentle dolphin eye. They would swim along on either side, then, at some silent signal, dart ahead on

both sides and leap across each other just ahead of the
bow of the boat. Who does the choreography for dolphin
dances, I wondered?

Then the wind shifted and I had to tack. The dolphins
continued straight ahead, heading for the mouth of the
cape to feed. In a minute, they were a quarter of a mile
from us. My heart sank in me. I wanted more contact. I felt
terribly unfinished. I began singing to my dolphin friends
in a way that I have found they relate to. As soon as I began
singing, I saw their dorsal fins turn 180 degrees and here
they were swimming back to us! In what seemed like an
instant, they were surrounding the boat again, squealing
their high-pitched song and rubbing against the boat.

I was in heaven! I was so happy, so ecstatic, that I said
to my son, "Take the rudder, Mike, I'm goin' in!" And, off
the boat I rolled, right into the middle of this glorious pod
of dolphins which had now grown from the original eight
to at least twelve. For an eternity of minutes we played together, we thrashed and splashed and laughed together.
I would hang on to the fin of a larger dolphin and it would
dive with me in tow. Just when I was certain my lungs
would give out, up we'd come, breaking the surface with
squeals and yells, my body all arms and legs flapping
wildly through the air, the dolphin's body a sleek arc of
graceful silver in the sun.

Now this, this is joy! I have never felt so full, so completely nourished in my life. Then I took notice of a
thought in my head. It was one of those "thoughts-in-my-
head-that-is-not-my-thought" that I have come to recognize as the way these wondrous beings communicate with
me. I am quite clear that the dolphin who was beside me
was sending me this message. The message was, "Be with
us."

"Be with us?" What is this dolphin talking about? Is it
crazy? "Be with us?" Why, I'm totally here, totally present
to this incredible moment. But the message comes again,
"Be with us, Danaan." Again, I resist it. "Hell, fella', I'm
here. I'm so happy and full and content; there's nowhere
else I'd rather be." And again comes the message, "Be
with us."

We're swimming slowly now, just gliding along with no effort, and I allow myself to stop defending my position. I listen, not just to the dolphin, but also to my own head. Then, I get it. Now I know what they're talking about. Now I can hear the game that's going on in my head. Slowly, I become aware of a "movie" that I am playing on the VCR in my brain. The movie plays on even in the midst of the joy of relating to the dolphins. In fact, the movie is playing because *of the joy I'm experiencing. The movie is entitled, "Isn't it awful what humans do to dolphins."*

There it is, playing on the wrap-around screen in my head, in full color. In this movie are all the scenes I have ever witnessed, or been told about, which document human's cruelty to dolphins: scenes from my standing on a dock in San Diego and seeing the fishing boats return from sea with drowned dolphins caught in the gill-nets, scenes from my witnessing Japanese fishermen shooting dolphins because they were thought to be competing for their catch of fish, scenes of confined dolphins being taught to retrieve dummy — and sometimes transport live — torpedos for the Navy. All this is going on in my head and I'm beginning to allow this movie and the guilt that is generated by it to separate me from my dolphin friends and this exquisite moment.

And my friends are saying, "Be with us, Danaan. Yes," they say, "we know about all of that, but that is there and we, you and we, are here. Be here, Danaan, don't use that to separate yourself from us."

And I realize that what I am doing with the dolphins, I also do other places in my life. It isn't the BAD moments I have so much trouble with; it's the really GOOD moments. When it gets too good, too nourishing, when the possibility of JOY gets too close, then I pop a video tape into the VCR in my head to give me a little separation from all that ecstasy. I'll let myself be, perhaps, 85% present to the good but not 100% because that means surrender. That means letting go. Being in-between trapezes is still a scary place to be. Thank you, brother/sister dolphins, you truly are my teachers.

Well, my human friends, I say to you and I say to me that our planet cries out for us to be 100% present. Being 100% present to the moments in our lives is *the* most powerful tool you and I have to make our lives work. That's right. No technique, no communication skill or psychological process can come anywhere close to the effectiveness of being 100% present. It is not an easy thing to do.

There are two situations where it is very important for the Warrior of the Heart to be that fully present. One situation is in the midst of conflict and the other is in the presence of the possibility of joy. I have noticed it is exactly in these two situations that most of us "run-away," either physically or psychologically. In fact, our entire cultural training actually teaches us to run-away from these moments of intensity. It provides us with an endless array of diversions and substitutes for this personally experienced intensity, as if we have created all of our cultural structures, all our educational processes, all our methods of human-to-human interaction so as to isolate ourselves from one another in those moments, either "positive" or "negative," which have the potential for *intensity* and, more importantly, *intimacy.*

Intensity, Intimacy And Really Seeing Others

So, there it is, that magic word that holds the key to being 100% present. Intimacy. It is the one thing in human interaction that moves us from the position of adversaries to that of co-creators. Intimacy is the one element that shifts band-aid problem solving into true conflict resolution. It is the necessary ingredient in transforming win/lose, me-against-you competition into win/win, cooperative and creative peacemaking. Isn't it interesting that our whole society is set up to keep us from really experiencing intimacy? Isn't it fascinating that intimacy scares almost all of us silly?

A few months ago, I gave a series of lectures in Southern California. With a day off in between, a friend and I decided to go to Disneyland. I loved the Matterhorn with its water toboggan run and the haunted house with its hologram ghosts, but there was always that feeling of plastic vicariousness that is present in a place made to look like something it isn't. On the "riverboat," a simulation of an old Mississippi stern-wheeler, its "stern wheel" splashing uselessly as an underwater cable pulls the boat along, I heard a young couple say, "This is great.

Why go to all the trouble to see New Orleans? They've brought it here to us!" Of course. Why experience the real thing when we can have its plastic effigy to experience without all that realness, without that potential for something, or someone, unexpected to happen.

We have created a plastic-coated Disneyland of simulated intensity, of artificial intimacy, and it's called 20th century society. Within it we are safe to vicariously explore, to "view" all the passion and depth and feeling in the world from the safety of our armchairs while still remaining securely ensconced in the cultural mediocrity that isolates us from the *change process*. How safe it is and how dead.

But what about *you*? What about the person who is beginning to extricate her/himself from the bog of cultural mediocrity? What about the Warrior of the Heart who knows that *intensity* is the fuel for change, the juice, the Ki of life? Who knows that *intimacy* is the secret force that turns mediocre, surface relationships into deep, healing, peace-filled relationships? How does *this* person make the switch?

Listen to the dolphins.

We have been programmed to respond with deadness to the two most important moments in our lives - the moments of conflict and the moments of ecstasy. Don't do that! Be 100% present to those precious moments. When you become aware that there is a conflict in your life, when you feel yourself begin to run away or begin to attack as a way of defending your position, stop. Breathe. Use your *will* to call upon all your internal forces to be totally present to this situation. *Be* there, 100%. In the clarity of that 100% presence, you will see what it is you are to do next. In the presence of actual, not simply projected, physical danger, your next step may be to remove yourself from that environment. But most likely, the clarity of your 100% presence to the conflict will, in itself, begin the process of resolution.

Being there 100% means much more than not attacking or running away (fight or flight). It means:

1) *Allowing yourself* to really experience what is occur
   ring here and now instead of drowning in a pool of
   images of past experiences.

2) Suspending your judgments. *Letting go of your position* so that you have the possibility of understanding someone else's position.

3) *Listening. Really listening*, not just gathering ammunition to re-attack with.

4) *Creating a safe space* inside yourself, an inner place that isn't reacting to survival signals from those thousands of fearful past experiences in your head.

When I say that 100% presence requires you to be *here* instead of immersed in images of past experience, what I'm talking about is this: *It is very difficult for anyone to see anyone else in the present moment.*
Why? Because:

A) Our medullas are letting through only that information which relates to survival issues.

B) Our cortex compares every piece of *new* experience to every piece of old information in our heads.

C) We humans seem to carry around a cast of characters in our heads and a library of old VCR tapes that consistently get in between us and the person we are trying to be present to, as if there were a cloud, a fog bank, in between us and the person we are trying to see clearly.

Some of this fog is put there by us and some of it is put there by the other person. The major dilemma of course, is that we usually do not *notice* the fog. We *think* we see each other clearly. But what we really see is just the dim outline of the other and mostly we see the reflection off of the water droplets in the fog bank. In a sense, we're mostly seeing distorted reflections of *ourselves* and our own projections and fantasies while thinking we clearly see the other person.

My old mentor in gestalt therapy told me a story about the time when he had just graduated from the Gestalt Institute and had set up a practice in San Francisco. He was an immediate success. He's a very sharp and caring man and people came from all over California to work with him.

After about one year, he decided that he would "take stock" of his practice and see who was coming to him for what. He discovered something interesting. His clientele represented all areas of psychological problems, except one. They came with every kind of problem, fear, dysfunction, etc., except - no one ever came to him with any type of sexual problem.

Well, he figured that the answer to this must be that there was a dynamite sex-therapist in the neighborhood and everyone with a sexual problem went to that specialist while everyone else came to him. Right? Wrong, of course!

A few months later, he was doing some "upgrading," as a participant in a workshop. In the midst of some didactic sharing with a fellow therapist, she stopped him and said, "John, I'd like to give you some feedback. First of all, I want to affirm you for your listening skills. It's really easy to share with you. Your body language is very positive, you have good eye contact, you gently encourage me to go deeper and I enjoy our contact. However, John, every time I bring up anything that has to do with my sexuality - all the blood drains out of your face! *It's fascinating because nothing else changes. You still maintain eye contact, you're still a good listener, your body language stays open, but your face turns absolutely stark white and it looks like you're dying! And,"* she said, *"I get the clear message from you that it is not okay for me to talk about my sexuality with you. So, I immediately change the subject because I can feel your fear and I get fearful, too."*

At that moment, John was aware of why no one ever came to him for any sexually related problem. In fact, they did come to him and he scared them away. Some "cloud" was being placed, by him, between him and his clients.

Awareness is always a major part of the solution. John's new awareness allowed him to explore his problem more deeply. In the process of some breathing therapy which focused on this issue, he had an image appear in his mind. It was the image of him at about eight years old in his room. His mother came bursting into the room and caught him masturbating. She did not handle the situation delicately and he decided, right then and there, to not deal with sexuality ever again. Actually, he made two decisions. One was to not deal with sexuality. The other decision was to forget that he made the first decision. (These kinds of decisions do usually come in pairs.)

Thirty years and three marriages later, he was now prepared to upgrade his decisions so that he could truly "see" people and not just the cloudy ghosts of his past experiences.

I too have had experiences that have taught me how difficult it is to be *here and now*, relating to the real people who are in front of us, instead of the ghosts and projections we use to keep ourselves safe and to "make sense" of our world.

When I first opened a private clinical practice, I quickly learned that every woman who came into my office who was over 60 and had any kind of alcoholic problem immediately became my mother. I would sit there for an hour listening to them, making comments. All the time I wasn't present to this real life human being, I was dealing with my dead mother whose alcoholic behavior had left me with tons of unresolved baggage of my own. Pretty good, huh? Charging them $60 an hour so I could do therapy with my mother? No way. Nobody won on that one and I had to stop seeing clients with that profile until I myself could clean up my act.

Another incident occurred just a year ago while I was giving a lecture to a large group in San Francisco. After my talk, a small group of folks came up to ask questions, shake my hand and say hi.

About the fourth person in line was a young woman who came up and hugged me and said that she thoroughly enjoyed my talk. In fact, she said, "You said something that changed my life." When I asked what that was and she told me, I sheepishly had to tell her that I had not said that! It was a good thing to say and I'll probably say it someday. But I didn't say it that night.

The very next man in line approached me gruffly and said, "You have got to be the biggest ass I've ever heard. Why, how could you say _____?" Guess what? I never said that, either!

I thought to myself, "Hello, is there anybody out there?" Are there any real live people talking to real live people on this planet or are there just a bunch of movies playing on projection screens everywhere?

You and I, we have a responsibility that needs to be honored. If you wish to claim that Warrior of the Heart that is yearning to be set free inside of you, then you will accept the responsibility for sweeping away that fog bank, that cloud of old energies and ghosts that prevent you from seeing clearly. One of the ways of describing the Warrior of the Heart is that he or she is a "people person." Although each of us manifests this trait in our own unique way, it's as if we all hang out our shingle which says *people person* on it. It means we make ourselves available. We say to our world, "I'm here. You can count on me to be present to you, to see you clearly beyond the fog and to encourage you to blow away your fog, too." This is a great gift that you give to your world and to the furtherance of planetary peace.

In my work in international conflict resolution, which at times takes me into situations of violent conflict, I have found it useful to actually verbalize my commitment to being 100% present to the conflict. I find myself saying, many times out loud, "I am here." That simple statement has become a signal to my nervous system to *not* go on "fight or flight." It has become a lightning swift message to my medulla and my bio-computer/cerebral cortex that I'm going to see this one through, so for your own survival, guys, you better supply me with the information I need, in the ways I can use it, to accomplish what I'm about to do. In those moments, I can feel the thousands of diverse elements in my body begin to pull together as a team. My brain, my mind, my nervous system, my endocrine glands, my electric field, every cell in my body go "on-line" and know integration of purpose. It's a wonderful feeling. Moreover, it is a powerful experience of *re-programming* away from fight or flight survival of our ancestors and toward the awareness of interdependence and unity of evolutionary purpose that we will need to become 21st century humans.

Exercise

Please think about those situations in your life where you have a difficult time "being present." We all have them and your calling them into awareness allows you to grow from them.

You know the situations I refer to, the ones where your body is there, but you have a hard time staying focused. You feel like you are not being real, your mind clouds over, you want to be somewhere else, you try to make conversation but it comes out like mush.

See if you can identify two of those situations:

#1. The scene:

Who's there?

What are you feeling?

How does it end?

#2. The scene:

Who's there?

What are you feeling?

How does it end?

In either of these situations, what are the issues around "intimacy" in that encounter? What's really going on? *Why* do you feel like you want to "go out to lunch?"

What are some ways that you could stay more "present" to those situations?

(I use things like deep breathing, eye contact, sharing my feelings, owning my difficulty while trying to explore together some "source conflicts" behind the "presenting problem," sharing my fear, my doubts, my hopes, my confusion.)

Sometimes I have a hard time being present to my kids or my partner. I always have a hard time being present to my ex-wife or anyone I feel threatened by. When I can muster the courage to take positive action in that situation, we both win. Deep down, every one of us has a desire to *be real* with others. It's just too scary to admit it sometimes. But it feels so good when we do something about it.

I remember a class I taught years ago in Berkeley. There was one person in that class who talked incessantly about nothing it seemed. Everyone spent incredible amounts of time and energy avoiding this person because to be "caught" was worse than death.

One day after class, I got caught. Pinned against the blackboard, I felt myself beginning to psychologically go "out to lunch" just to survive emotionally. I started thinking about what to buy at the grocery store, about the papers I had to grade, all kinds of fantasies. All the while I nodded understandingly to my attacker with an occasional and random uh-huh for effect.

He went on and on. I ran out of fantasies. Something in me said, "Stop running, Danaan. BE here!" How can I be here for him and still take care of me? "Tell your truth." Okay!

I just said what was my truth. Not THE truth, just my truth. I said, "Frank, I've got to tell you what's going on with me. I'm BORED! That doesn't mean that you are boring, just that I feel bored, and I want to do something about it so that you and I can have a more meaningful conversation right now. Can we talk about what's going on here that winds up with me feeling bored? That would be a very interesting subject for me."

Silence. Then he said, "Thank you. Thank you for caring enough to stay and say your truth and still be here." What transpired after that was a wonderful conversation which covered everything from my problems with saying what's true for me to his terror about nobody listening to him so he bores them to death to validate his fear-fantasy. I was anything but bored.

That simple statement of "how-it-is-for-me" transformed our relationship and gave us each a chance to look at our next steps in personal growth as well. Tell your truth and transform your life!

4

SAFE SPACE

Chapter 15

Safe Space

One of the most challenging assignments I have ever accepted brought me to Pakistan, to see if there was some way of bringing together the peoples of two opposing religious beliefs, Pakistani Christians and Pakistani Moslems. Especially in the mountain city of Murree, violence had been a way of relating for these groups and much blood had been spilled on both sides.

When we arrived in the midst of this seemingly hopeless situation, we began to explore the possibility of "common ground" or areas where a common value or belief or need might be present. It was in speaking with the teachers of the different upper schools (high schools) that a common need was expressed. They all wished that they had counselling skills! They had all read books about counselling and had heard of the benefit to students of guidance counselling and personal counselling but no one had ever had training in this field. AHA!

To make a long and crazy story shorter, let me just say that we arranged for as many of the teachers in Murree to receive counselling training as wanted it. There was only one stipulation - the classes were half Christian teachers and half Moslem teachers. For five weeks, in the evenings, Christian and Moslem teachers were in the same space to get what each wanted more than they were revolted by the presence of "the other." Most of them had never been in the same room with "them" before, although they lived only blocks away.

How do you teach counselling skills? Experientially, of course. You don't just lecture about it; you involve the whole class in exercises. You do role-playing, psychodrama. You form into diads (couples) and small groups. You interact.

We were creating a safe space. Safe spaces don't just happen because you get a bunch of people in a room together. We taught them listening skills and had them practice them, one Moslem and one Christian. We taught them about I-messages, about feedback, body language and group dynamics. We were the experiment. We were the laboratory.

Sometimes, to create a safe space, you need to turn the energy away from the conflicted parties (A), and focus it on a third point (B), as in this diagram:

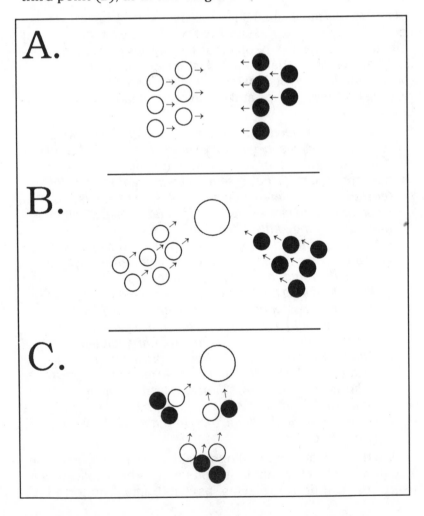

If the groups and the individuals are feeling listened to and respected, and if the third point of focus is relevant and has integrity, then maybe, just maybe, the opposing groups can be gently moved together to create a single group which relates to the focus point as in (C).

In this Pakistani group it did happen and the element that supplied the magic was one that I have seen work over and over again. The magic was in the sharing of their pain.

It started by focusing our sharing exercises on the grief that each group was feeling. At first, it took the form of a contest:

"Your people killed my brother."

"Yes, but that was because your people burned our buildings."

Then,

"I hurt so much because you killed my brother; I miss him so deeply."

Then,

"I am in constant pain; my life knows only grief."

When they could listen to each other, they heard that they *all* were in this grief. There was no one who was not deeply wounded. In that darkness and despair, there was no "other," only hurting people in search of healing.

We asked them to make a sound to express their feeling. A wail, a grief-filled moan filled the room as if from one voice. It continued for an hour and when it subsided, a Christian was laying in the lap of a Moslem; a Moslem was cradled by a Christian; an old man and a young boy, once enemies, stared into each other's eyes and saw themselves.

Somehow, through some cosmic quirk of fate, we humans are able to come together in our grief where we cannot come together in our joy. So be it. We can use it to create a safe space within which to heal our planet.

Chapter 16

Ground Rules

It may sound a bit stiff and formal but ground rules are important in the creation of a safe space. It's your job to communicate them and to get agreement in a way that keeps it from feeling oppressive and coercive. Ground rules will differ from situation to situation but these are quite standard to most situations:

A. *No physical violence.* No psychological/emotional violence is also a rule for 99% of conflict resolution. But, in the case of Christians and Moslems in Pakistan or the IRA/UVF in Northern Ireland and even in some domestic situations, one must tolerate and work with abusive behavior if it remains physically non-violent and if the mediator can get agreement as to the "equal-time" rule.

B. *Equal time.* Quite simply, one party agrees to listen and not interrupt while the other is speaking with the guarantee that they will have an equal opportunity to speak and be listened to.

C. *Active listening.* All parties agree to simply and correctly paraphrase the main points of the other party's communication prior to beginning their equal time communication. The first party must agree that their main points have been heard (not necessarily agreed with, just heard). Then, it's time for the second party to speak and the first party to listen and then paraphrase the communication to the second party's satisfaction.

This equal time sharing goes back and forth until everyone feels heard and all main points are out in the open. Then, we move to an exploration of options.

It is the mediator's job to be listening for:

a) *Sourcing conflicts lying beneath presenting problems.*

1. Mention their existence and try to have the parties incorporate them into their equal time sharing.

2. Be willing to be wrong about the presence of a sourcing conflict and let go of your "position" on it.

b) *Areas of common ground.*

1. Places where the conflicted parties share a common view of reality, a common "truth."

2. Bring these up in the next step.

D. *Willingness to explore options.*

A safe space needs everyone's permission to ex plore, to brainstorm, to fantasize options and alternative solutions which no one has even thought about yet. In this way you can develop excitement about co-creating wonderful, fresh, expanded possibilities which embody the potential for win/win outcomes for all concerned.

E. *Confidentiality.*

In a safe space, all parties need to know that what they share there will stay there. You must seek agreement to the ground rules that what is said inside this space is privileged information for our ears only. Finding agreement on this ground rule can sometimes take time and be hard at first, since participants have wives, husbands, business partners, etc. who will want to know what has occurred. Nevertheless you need to uncover those sensitive areas which demand confidentiality and get agreement that *those* topics won't be discussed outside this safe space.

F. *Commitment to Stay.*

As I've said before, we are taught from birth to avoid conflict. When things get hot, some folks want to split. After introducing the idea that conflict *IS*, that it's a natural outcome of more than one human being inhabiting this planet and that you can't have *conflict*-resolution without conflict, then you are ready to seek agreement on the ground rule "commitment to stay." Each party needs to know that the others aren't going to bolt. The commitment needed to support a safe space is usually to stay until the session is over, requiring you to set some quitting time. It's usually a good idea to get a further commitment to one or more sessions at which time we re-negotiate this commitment.

STOP

Here are a few of the things you and I need to *stop* doing if we want to create a *safe space*:

1. *Stop* assuming that your truth is *the* truth. What is true for you is not necessarily true for another.

2. *Stop* insisting that other people must agree with you. Disagreement is okay. Don't "cross-examine" people.

3. *Stop* unconsciously assuming that anyone else will see it the way you see it. Always check it out.

4. *Stop* invalidating other people's experience just because it doesn't agree with your experience.

5. *Stop* blaming anyone else for how you feel or what happens to you. Take full responsibility for yourself.

Chapter 17

Techniques

Here are a few techniques for creating and maintaining a "safe space."

ATTUNED BREATHING

It's the oldest trick in the book. When people get conflicted and feel attacked, they hold their breath. Or, they take shallow, short breaths which only get to their upper chest or bronchial area. Their energy gets blocked, fear rises, protection and resistance result.

Breathe. Breathe deep and long. Make a soft, gentle sound when you breathe; let your chest and belly expand and contract with each in-breath and out-breath. As you breathe, you are modelling breathing. You are re-minding people to choose life and to nourish themselves. This creates a safe space.

Further, you should endeavor to create "attuned breathing." It *is* possible to get everyone breathing in rhythm and this is a powerful way to unite the group beyond surface disagreement.

After you've modelled breathing and it's catching on, you'll notice that many people in the room are already breathing in the same rhythm. You must be a very observant student of body language to see/feel this pattern. Support this rhythm with your own breathing and body movement. Keep it up even as you direct the many other activities necessary, even as you speak.

We are all like pendulums in this regard. Start a bunch of pendulums swinging randomly and come back a while later to find that they are all swinging in resonance. Given a little help and encouragement, we will all move towards resonance with each other, breathing, swaying, dancing to the natural harmony that unites us beneath the surface "positions" that separate us.

LISTENING

Again, you are a model for how to create a safe space. Listening, real listening, like breathing, can be contagious.

Real listening isn't just done with your ears; it's done with every cell of your being. It demands that each molecule of you becomes an earphone, a receiver. You pick up information at the cellular level, at the psychic/intuitive level, at the emotional level. Only a small part of incoming information is picked up by your ears. Listen with *all* of you.

Sit upright yet relaxed with your feet on the floor and your arms unfolded. Make eye contact with the person who is speaking but don't stare. A slight head gesture, made appropriately, conveys not agreement but comprehension.

Don't try to seduce the speaker. Inappropriate gestures or facial expressions of approval or disapproval convey manipulative messages of, "Keep on *that* track and I'll support you" or "Boy, that's a stupid thing to be talking about." Just *be there*, like with a pod of dolphins as they share their wonderful mysteries with you.

To be there, listening 100% with your transmitter turned down and your receiver turned way up, requires you to momentarily surrender all of your *positions* and all of your *absolute* truths about how it is. It requires you to open up to someone else's truth, even at the risk of having to change your mind, maybe even change your life. And they wonder why we call it the Warrior of the Heart!

ASKING QUESTIONS

Better you should just *listen.*

But, if you must ask questions, remember this:

1. Questions usually cause defensiveness. Always tell people *why* you need the answer to a question and ask "open-ended" questions, ones that don't only require a "yes" or "no" answer. Let people answer in their own words.

2. Appreciate the silence. Silence is powerful communication. Let it be when it happens, either with yourself or others. Resist the need to fill the silence with words.

3. Ask general, inviting questions. Let your questions be permission for people to explore feelings and new ways of seeing things.... "Would you tell me how you really feel about what just happened and I'll listen?"

4. Help people to access deeper levels of communication. "Everyone has difficulty talking about feelings (or about _____). I do. My difficulty is _____ . Can you tell me where the difficulty is for you?"

5. Summarize what has been said and check it for accuracy, then ask your question.

6. Use questions to offer alternatives that are open-ended. "Do you think we could get some counseling about this?" "Is there a way for us both to get what we want?"

7. The cardinal rule for asking questions is: Give something of yourself before you demand anything of someone else. If you want to know what's going on for another person, then tell them what is going on with you first. Only then do you have the right to ask your question.

DO SOMETHING TOGETHER

The rule of thumb is: If you want to create a safe space for people in conflict, get them to *DO* something together, cooperatively. Don't just talk.

Talking keeps people locked up in their heads. For lasting resolution, people have to "get it" in their entire body-mind system. Furthermore, when people cooperate on small tasks, they are psychologically better prepared to cooperate on resolving their conflicts.

One of the reasons why my organization does so much tree planting around the world is that we have found, time after time, that planting trees together is a powerful psychological act of bonding for those involved. So we use reforestation and desert reclamation projects as a vehicle for groups in conflict to come together. As they get muddy and sweaty together, they begin to relate to each other outside of the limited boundaries of their preconceived stereotypes. Planting a tree is creating a living symbol of hope. It says, "We who did this acknowledge that there is meaning in the world beyond me and my problems, us and our problems." It is an act of faith in the future. It is a shared act that creates a safe space.

Don't just talk; DO something together:

Rearrange the furniture

Create an agenda together

Make a drawing of your shared predicament

Do some role playing

Prepare lunch together

Plant trees, buy plants as a gift together

Share everyone's favorite stretching exercise

Take a walk together

Complain to the building manager about the noise, the paint job, the heat, whatever, together

Just do something and do it together

Chapter 18

Energy Flow

CIRCULAR ENERGY FLOW

Geometry: Always create circular geometries. Conflict resolution converts linear communication into circular communication. Even in my Pakistani example, the transformation could not occur until the focus is taken off the leader and distributed among the participants.

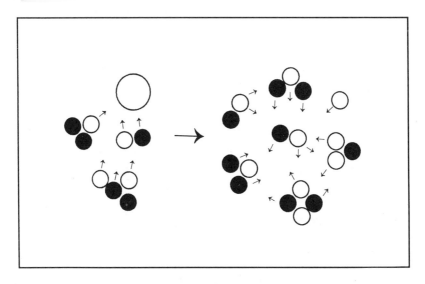

Only in this kind of safe space can people let go of their previously held "positions."

Sometimes, it's as simple as rearranging the group so that they/we sit in a circle with nothing separating us. When this is not possible, one has to create a dynamic flow of circular energy and communication with the group. This is where a study of the martial art of Aikido is valuable. The group leaders can imagine a swirling circular flow connecting and infusing the group and, by their questions, their eye contacts, their directed answers and the way they set up group activities, they can swirl the energy around and around the group.

Circular flow is equally important when only two people are interacting. Not only can you, as one of the two, visualize a circular pattern to the give and take of your communication, you can also remember the four elements needed for complete communication and employ them as a circle as you alternately speak and listen, speak and listen:

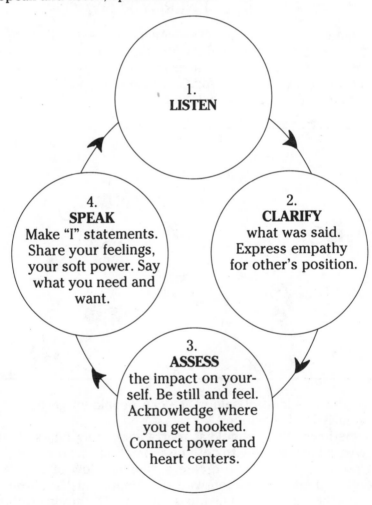

1.
LISTEN

2.
CLARIFY
what was said.
Express empathy
for other's position.

3.
ASSESS
the impact on your-
self. Be still and feel.
Acknowledge where
you get hooked.
Connect power and
heart centers.

4.
SPEAK
Make "I" statements.
Share your feelings,
your soft power. Say
what you need and
want.

TWO PERSON CIRCLES

We can adapt the concept of the circular flow of Ki in Aikido to the idea of creating a circular communication geometry even when there are only two communicating.

When you are communicating with another person, visualize that your communication starts not at your mouth (very little of our communication to another is verbal), but in your Hara, your power center. Bring the Ki up through your heart (where it is softened and infused with compassion) and out the top of your head (where your mind infuses it with understanding).

NB.

Imagine the communication, riding on the carrier of Ki, entering into your partner's mind where it is understood, down into her or his heart where it is received with compassion, and down into his or her Hara where it is experienced at the feeling level and where your Ki is received as a gift of pure energy. That Ki then continues on its circular path back to your Hara and the cycle is complete.

When your partner communicates to you, visualize this same cycle in reverse. Feel the communication entering your mind, go down to your heart and then to your Hara. Two things to watch for are:

1. Be sure to let the Ki pass *through* your Hara after you have silently thanked your partner for sharing it with you. Don't "hold on" to Ki; that's where real trouble starts. Let it flow.

   Remember, Aikido always looks upon the other person as a *partner* even if the other person is trying to attack you. The dances we do with different people may *look* very different but each person is still your dance partner.

2. If you feel your belly get tight when your partner communicates to you, it's because you have drawn the energy into your belly before bringing it through your mind and your heart. You have made it a *linear* flow and you need to re-establish the circular flow.

   It's great to practice this visualization with someone you care about (*before* conflict is present) and to verbalize what's going on in your head, your heart, and then your belly and let your partner do the same.

YOUR LIFE IS YOUR LABORATORY

Seek opportunities to observe and practice the concepts you have just read about. For instance, when you are in a group of people, begin noticing the different kinds and qualities of communication that go on. Watch two people talk to each other and notice where their communication "comes from" and "goes to." By that I mean not their words, which obviously go from ear to ear, but the real transfer of "communication energy." Does it go from Hara to Hara without passing through the Heart or the Head? Does it go from Head straight to Belly

(Hara) like a sword thrust, leaving the receiver feeling attacked? Or is there a circular flow as in the diagram on page 123.

Begin noticing how some people do listen to others and how most people aren't listening much at all but rather preparing their reply (or counterattack) while pretending to be listening. Notice their body language. Notice their eyes. Become a student of human behavior and you will learn all you need to know. Sit back and notice what works and what doesn't. Watch how people's bodies soften or harden to learn what does and doesn't work. A person's body will always tell you if the communication is getting through or not.

Listen to people assume "positions," take "stands" on certain issues. Watch their bodies when this happens and watch the bodies of the other persons involved. Just sitting in the corner and watching, really watching the show, can be a graduate course in effective and ineffective communication techniques.

Of course, the final exam is to develop the ability to "watch yourself" as you communicate and listen. If only we could have someone secretly videotape us as we go about our everyday communications, what an incredible learning experience it would be to study that video.

I suggest that you *can* develop the ability to watch yourself, to become conscious of how you act and react in your communications. You *can* put a little bit of your consciousness up in the "corner of the room" and it can be aware of what you do. Try it.

> NOTE: This book is not a course in professional mediation. If you are drawn to seek professional certification in the fields of mediation, dispute resolution, I recommend that you read a few of the books on the subject in the bibliography (let the first be *Getting to Yes* by Uri and Fischer) and then contact one of the many mediation centers in most cities for next steps.
>
> My intent here is to give you, the Warrior of the Heart, the needed information and awareness so that you can *live* your desire to be a co-creator of peaceful change in your life.

5

CHANGE

19
Anatomy
of the Change Process

20
Men and Women

21
Relationship
as a Warrior Path

Chapter 19

Anatomy of the Change Process

CREATIVE CHANGE

Another term for creative change is conflict resolution. By conflict resolution, I mean true resolution and not surface problem solving. In my definition of those terms, problem solving looks only at the presenting problem, the *issue*, and tries to find the best solution to that issue-oriented problem. Conflict resolution, when it works, not only solves the issue-related problem, it also heals the relationships involved. Because real peacemaking is accomplished at the relationship level, the "problem" won't stay solved for very long unless the relationships involved go through some sort of healing.

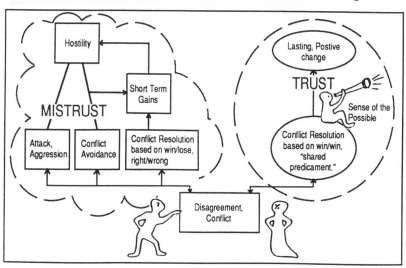

TEN POINTS TO REMEMBER

Here is a summary of my "ten points to remember" when you are given the opportunity to deal with CONFLICT:

1. Conflict is like breathing. There is no relationship without it. Recognize that conflict IS.

2. The presenting problem is almost never the real problem. Getting stuck in the former isolates you from yourself and others and prevents resolution.

3. To resolve conflict, you need to create a safe space. A safe space is one in which you feel free to share your vulnerabilities, knowing that you won't be judged, attacked or reacted to.

4. Conflict is about intimacy. To be intimate requires doing something that will get attention. Being human, we tend to create some kind of negativity in order to be noticed. The core of real connection is shared pain.

5. Change occurs right at the edge of your comfort zone. Our comfort zone is a place we go to heal, to relax, to be quiet. We need to step out beyond that zone to grow and to learn.

6. That which you resist, persists. Conflict seeks resolution, just as a discordant note in a melody seeks resolution. Sooner or later, you need to get to the root of the matter at hand.

7. You need to be 100% present in a conflict. This means you are not only physically, but also emotionally and mentally present. The more open you can be to your feelings, to what is happening around you, your responses and reactions, the more genuinely you can participate in the conflict at hand. Being present also involves letting go of preconceived images, outcomes and judgments, viewing and receiving whatever is happening here and now with a fresh set of eyes and an open heart.

8. Sex-related roles are an element of *every* conflict.

9. Guilt and fear block the resolution of conflict.

10. There are no absolute truths.

Demons As Allies
In Darkness Guard And Teach
Never Alone

Bebe

There is a secret that quantum physicists, aikido masters and those who work with basic energy have known for a long time — change occurs when polarities are integrated. Polarization opposes change.

Conflict resolution theorists say that if anyone loses, everyone loses. Win/lose really means lose/lose in the long run. For you to truly win in a lasting way, you must see to it that everyone involved feels, in some sense, like a winner.

CONFLICT RESOLUTION

Aikido masters say that opposing a negative force with your "positive" energy simply feeds the negative force. In other words, one should not oppose "evil," but transform it. To transform it, you must blend with it, honor it and co-create an outcome at a higher level of relationship than previously existed. For this, no less than the indomitable integrity of the warrior is called for.

Perhaps we can understand this more easily in our personal relationships than we can in our national conflicts.

When you and your partner or your child have a fight and you win the argument, do you really? What have you won? Will there not be resentment created that will reappear in some form? Have you not simply reinforced the polarities and actually inhibited true change?

Only when you co-create a closure wherein you both feel listened to, respected and valued can there be any hope of positive change in the relationship itself. This does not mean

that one of you has to be wrong. The creation of interdependent, mutually valued solutions can, in fact, only occur when
neither party has to feel wrong.

This presents quite a challenge to those of us who work in
the many areas of the peace movement. Our cause seems so
obviously right, so immediate, that it is easy to judge others as
"wrong" rather than to be of a different viewpoint. We are
challenged to move beyond this win/lose attitude, to identify
the foundation of common concern and agreement and to seek
solutions that honor the opinions and fears of others and
ourselves.

For example, everyone on all sides of the nuclear weapons
issue shares a common urge called survival. Every cell in every
being's body is geared to survival. When this organic, primal
need manifests outwardly, it takes the form of either competition or cooperation.

In his book, *Parable of the Tribes*, Andrew Schmookler says
that primitive tribes interacted in basically one of two ways -
warfare or gift-giving. So it is with us. It is sadly ironic that many
of the peace groups have chosen to utilize a warfare (adversary, win/lose) approach, rather than the gift-giving (alliance,
win/win) approach to accomplish their goals.

But, in all corners of the peace movement, a new breed of
activist is emerging who sees beyond the fear and the short-
term win/lose approach. This new change-maker is willing to
own his or her fear of not-surviving, but is not imprisoned by
that fear. S/he is working to create vehicles for win/win outcomes, identifying options that address the survival and security needs of those on both sides of the polarity.

Can you allow "them" to win, as long as you win, too?

Most people cannot. They still feel that their "opponent" has
to lose if they are to win. This is a false but deeply held belief
and one that perpetuates conflict. Real conflict resolution
demands win/win outcomes.

For people, groups or nations to achieve win/win solutions,
two elements are absolutely necessary. These elements are
trust, and what I will call " the sense of the possible."

TRUST

Without trust, we can forget positive change, forget peaceful interaction and, given the present state of our planet, forget survival. Regardless of our pictures of how rotten "he" is or "they" are or the "government" is or the "Soviets" are...we must find ways to co-create trust with exactly those people who generate feelings of mistrust within us. This may be some sort of cosmic humor, but it is also the only path to peace.

Trust grows out of contact. The development of trust requires familiarity; it demands that we open our rusty gates of suspicion and prejudice and righteousness, even if we were badly bruised when we last opened them. If this were an easy process, we would have already solved the problem.

The development of trust demands that we find unpolarized ways to be together. Working together on a task that we all validate as meaningful is the best way I know of building trust. Trust does not mean "I agree with you"; it means "I affirm who you are, even though I may not agree with what you do or think." Are you ready to open up that far?

THE SENSE OF THE POSSIBLE

Most efforts toward change come from a position of "Isn't it awful that...." It is time for us to try "Wouldn't it be wonderful if...." It is no longer enough to say no. We now must find ways to say as passionate a YES to what can be, as we say NO to what is. We must be moving toward something wonderful and not just away from something terrible. We must breathe life into our dreams.

I am not suggesting that saying no, that opposing oppression and violence, is no longer needed. We MUST have the courage to say no when no needs to be said. But surely it is possible to see that "opposing oppression" is a win/lose position and can only, at best, lead to short-term solutions. If you doubt this, reflect on every war that was ever fought to secure peace and examine the long-term outcome for the "winners" and "losers."

Let there always be a yes to balance each no. Let there now be a passionate commitment to a positive future when our no's have had their effect.

And, that *yes*, that movement towards the positive, must include everyone, even those to whom we said no. We must accept responsibility for solutions that have no losers, even when our "adversaries" are unwilling to participate in this. The state of our planet, the failure of old win/lose tactics calls us to move beyond winners and losers, victors and vanquished, and enter into an interdependent relationship with those whom we have previously labeled as adversary.

The term paradigm-shift has been used to describe the massive consciousness shift that has the possibility of happening in our lifetime. I believe what we have been addressing here is intimately tied to this shift away from winners and losers, us good-guys and those bad-guys, to a consciousness of interdependence and we-ness. This sounds like a small shift, but I believe it is the one puzzle piece which could trigger the next evolutionary quantum-leap, the awareness that you and I are parts of a greater living whole. You may say that you already possess the awareness of wholism. Remember that assertion the next time your mate violates your ego boundaries and you revert to "you/me" defense tactics. We only know the concept intellectually. However, we're getting close to experiencing it, and the exciting thing is that the chaos and the strong polarization now pressing on us have been the very mechanisms that have forced us to this next "edge-of-consciousness."

We now have the choice. I choose YES.

> **"They were told "NO" a thousand times**
> **and after the final "NO" there was**
> **a "YES" that saved the world."**
> *Wallace Stevens*

Exercise

IDENTIFYING YOUR YES

Take a few moments to go inside and quiet down so that you can connect with that sense of "YES" that calls to you.

There lives in you a "sense of the possible," a yearning to move forward to embrace life in all its fullness. It's time to identify that "YES-to-Life" in you so that it will draw itself to you.

Put your feet on the floor, sit with your back straight and bring your hands together in your lap. Now before you close your eyes, here's what I want you to do with your eyes closed. Take full, deep breaths so that your chest rises and falls noticeably. Slowly separate your hands and bring your elbows back so that finally your elbows are pointing behind you. This pulls your shoulders back and causes your chest to open up. The idea is to slowly cause your lung cavity to open wide, and your heart to open, too. Keep breathing deeply.

As this opening slowly happens, with your eyes closed, allow yourself to imagine that your whole being is opening to that sense of YES inside of you. You are letting your YES come out after years of NO. Don't think about what the YES is, just breathe it out into the open through your heart. Do this for a few minutes, then open your eyes.

When you have completed that, write what wants to be written down here. Just start writing and see what comes out. Don't judge it or yourself.

I SAY *YES* TO ...

I SAY *YES* TO ...

I SAY *YES* TO ...

i say yes

i say YES to my life

i say YES to love

i say YES to a one-world-
        family
i say YES to a planet at peace

i say YES to all the children
        everywhere
i say YES to us

i want my next act
   to increase the YES in the world

                                                    ð. p.

Try saying this aloud each day, from the heart,
            and watch it become true.

Chapter 20

Men and Women

"SOURCE CONFLICTS"/ "PRESENTING PROBLEMS"

"Some day, men and women will rise, they will
reach the mountain peak, they will meet big and
strong and free, ready to receive, to partake and to
bask in the golden rays of love. What fancy, what
imagination, what poetic genius can foresee even
approximately the potentialities of such a force in the
lives of men and women."

Emma Goldman

To truly be involved in conflict resolution, where we facilitate the resolution of the deep "source conflicts" that affect our lives and not just slap band-aids on surface "presenting problems," we must ask the really hard, deep questions.

As I go about my work in international conflict resolution, I try to ask, "What is the underlying nature of conflict in general? Why are human beings so hostile; why have we been killing each other, hurting each other for as long as there have been human beings?"

Many answers are given associated with fear of personal survival, belief in scarcity, the territorial imperative and societal definitions of "success," "power", and what is "desirable," etc. But there is one underlying dynamic, one source-conflict that shows itself in *every* conflict situation, in every culture. It is the dynamic that exists between *men* and *women*.

Whoever and whatever else the protagonists in a conflict are, they are always also men and men or women and women or women and men. This ingredient is one of the most powerful determinants of how the scenario will unfold because we women and men carry around with us a repertoire of postures, positions, pictures and prejudices related to "how a man acts," "how a woman should respond," "how men 'are' with men," etc., etc. This role-playing, mostly unconscious, bypasses the true resolution of conflict and keeps most people trapped in B-grade movie roles even in their most intimate relationships.

Learning about sex roles in Belfast

A few summers ago, I was in Belfast arranging a trip for Catholic and Protestant teenagers to visit the USA. This required that I negotiate with the various para-military groups there. I made some friendships during the negotiation process.

One of the members of an IRA group invited me to his home for supper and I gladly accepted, as this was an opportunity to experience the family life of the people I was working with.

As I sat at their supper table and later in front of the peat fire with them, I learned a great deal about the male-female, male-male and female-female dynamics and rules of the subculture. I remember most the role definition that was assigned to the young mother and wife in this IRA home. She was in charge of telling her children the stories of hatred. Yes, that was her duty and there was no way to question it - no women's support group to go to to get another view on it. So, night after night, this woman was required to keep the fear and resentment alive in her children. I sat there and listened while she said, "Sean, Patrick, don't ya' ever forget: it's those Protestants in the Shankill who keep our lives in misery. They hung your uncle, boys, and they'll get you, too, if you don't get 'em first." (Their uncle was killed twenty years ago, long before they were born.) "It's those Prods who have kept your father out of work and on the dole for the last eight years and they'll do it to you, so you'll always be on the hand-out with no respect to call your own. The only thing we've got left is our pride and honor, boys. Make the Prods pay for what they've done."

So the historical resentment is passed on to another generation. No more than one week later, I got invited to another home for dinner, except this time it was by a UVF (Ulster Volunteer Force) member. It was in the Protestant section of Belfast, the Shankill District. It was only eight blocks away from the Catholic family's house. It looked like the same house to me, almost looked like the same family. But it was on the "other" side of Falls Road and so it was separated by light-years of hatred.

Again, I sat and listened as this young mother fulfilled her role as the teller-of-the-hate-stories. Except this time, the enemy lives on the other side of Falls Road over in Andersontown and New Barnsley. Far into the night, the woman lived out one of her roles: "Michael, Patricia, you must never let those Catholics get near you. They're evil, hateful people. They burned your father and me out of our house before you were born and they'll shoot ya' for the fun of it. Keep 'em where they belong and always defend our honor and our rights, kids." Here, too, the children get taught to hate someone they do not know.

The roles that women and men play out in these painful situations is part and parcel of the violence and "stuckness" they live with. During that visit, I went into the center of Belfast to do some shopping at the department stores. In those years, you had to get a "body search" before you could enter the downtown center to make sure that you didn't have some dynamite strapped to you to blow up a store. There I was with my hands in the air while a young British soldier searched me and another pointed a submachine gun at me. As I looked into the eyes of these two young men, I saw their fear, their terror. They were trembling. I said, "Why are you so afraid? What are you afraid of? Certainly not me; you've got the gun."

What came pouring out of them was the story of what it's like to be a "man" in that culture. How you've got to stay tough and ready to get them before they get you. You can't trust anyone and never, never let them see your fear or your softness. They told me about how the army teaches them to turn their fear into hatred and direct that hatred out against the enemy. Hatred and anger (and fear) were the only repertoire of feeling/responses allowed if you wanted to survive. Oh God, how these young men were trapped in their roles of "what it's like to be a man."

Until we can grow beyond these artificial roles and begin to embrace the deeper beauty and strength of what it is *really* like to be a woman, to be a man, we are *all* chained to the wheel of "surface" petty hurt and "surface" petty pleasures of those who wear a mask and pretend to be real.

In our own American culture, we are beginning to ask some questions about the roles we are stuck in. We are only in kindergarten but at least we've started school. We have a long way to go to graduation. But where to go and how?

"Personality Me" and "Natural Me"

I've got this idea in my head about how I "learned to be a man." What I mean is that I sometimes experience *two* men in me. One is the natural man that I just *am* because I've got the appropriate genitalia, the prescribed quota of male hormones and lots of facial hair, etc. Yes, I definitely fall within the borders of the definition of "man."

But I experience *another* man in me and this is the man that I "learned to be." Sometimes, these two guys are very different men. Sometimes they feel like they're at war with each other. The *natural-man* in me did not have to learn to be a man, he just *is*. But my culture felt it necessary to *teach* me how to be a man and frankly, I do not appreciate most of what I was taught. My inner voice is telling me to go back and re-discover that natural man who has been covered over by the "man I learned to be" (I call this guy the Personality Man). Many of my women friends are embarking on this same journey: to re-discover their natural woman beneath the "woman they learned to be." This, I believe, is a vital journey to wholeness that we do for *all* our brothers and sisters. This is Warrior's work.

The Journey to Wholeness

Whatever else we are as humans, we are also men and women and we must bring consciousness to this aspect of our being. Much is being said about our need for integration of masculine and feminine. As we men become more aware of ourselves, we seem to develop a natural desire to know the "feminine" aspects of our being: our gentle, soft, receptive, intuitive nature. This yearning to know wholeness also draws women to experience their "masculine" side: their linear, causal, assertive, rational nature. There is movement towards balance from both sides. This willingness, this desire to know the fullness of ourselves beyond the old cultural models, is one of the most positive and solid aspects that I have seen in what we are calling the age of transformation.

I prefer to use YANG and YIN rather than masculine and feminine. Yang (our outer do-ing nature) and Yin (our inner being nature) are qualities which both women and men possess and it is the balance of these qualities which lead us all to deeper parts of our being to be truly transformative.

As with all journeys in consciousness, there are many levels to this movement. Because we humans are so eager to "make it happen," we can easily attach ourselves to the surface aspects of this movement in consciousness while ignoring the deeper parts – parts which must be included for the movement. What are the deeper aspects of maleness and femaleness? I would characterize three broad areas of development in the following way:

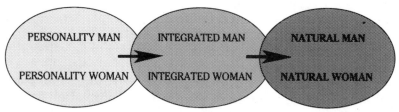

Certainly, the macho, hostile behaviors of most current male cultural stereotypes (Personality Man) need to change. This can be, and in many ways is being, balanced by men who are allowing the YIN aspects (that each of us men already have within us) to emerge and enrich our lives. In women, the old roles of victim and the "cute-but-helpless" manipulative behaviors (Personality Woman) are being balanced by women who are claiming their power and allowing their YANG aspects to integrate into themselves.

When this integration of our polarities has been accomplished, is there anything further? Is androgyny the "end point" of the journey for women and men? I think not.

I believe that *beneath* this outer male/female balance lies a more primary power source that must have the means of expression for wholeness to be experienced. Robert Bly calls it the "Wildman" in men. Only a woman can say what to call it in women; perhaps the "witch" in its ancient, positive connotation. I choose to call these deeper sources "natural woman" and "natural man."

The MALE Journey to Wholeness

As in my simple diagram, the path to wholeness for today's *man* leads him first away from ego performance and towards the be-ing aspect of the YIN nature that lies inside every male. This surface male do-ing aspect is the stuff of ego-personality. Personality Man acts to gain affirmation. His inadequate self-image imprisons him in doing, in his attempt to be loved. The integration of his YIN nature allows his inner voice to be heard in the quiet of being. This inner guidance will be the key in his ability to focus and creatively direct his primal energies during the next step in his journey, namely that of owning the natural maleness that lies deep within his body.

It is at this point of integration of YIN that we find many men losing their direction - and their spark. We males have been playing the role of the tough, invulnerable big-shot so long that when we give ourselves permission to just be, to be vulnerable and soft and not-in-charge, we then want to stay in this world of be-ing. It's such a relief not to have to keep up our flimsy acts of bravado! And, our sisters give us much affirmation for our new-found gentleness and ability to listen.

But there is more work to do, my brothers. There awaits the re-discovery of our male source, if we are willing to do the necessary work of putting away the old roles and stereotypes and allowing our deeper nature to emerge. It will happen *naturally* when we no longer need to play those ego games. Involvement in an ongoing men's group provides a great start to challenging the old roles and games. Remember that the deeper aspects of *natural* maleness will show themselves in as many unique ways are there are men, so don't try to cram your brothers into one definition of what "man" is, especially at our deeper levels of maleness.

VIOLENCE COMES NOT FROM ANY INNATE MASCULINE DRIVE, BUT RATHER FROM THE *DENIAL* OF THE DEEPEST LEVELS OF OUR MASCULINITY.

At this point I want to share an awareness that has come from my immediate experience in Belfast. As I open myself to the men of Belfast and to the daily violence and hostility of their lives, I am filled with the sense that violence comes *not* from any innate masculine drive but rather from the *denial*, the *imprisoning* of the deepest levels of our masculinity. In bullet-ridden Belfast, the men involved in the conflict do not allow themselves to experience either their inner YIN guidance or their deep masculine sureness and so they must find their sense of meaning in outer bravado.

Just as a steam boiler will violently erupt when its steam is not allowed to flow, so too our inner creative nature erupts violently when it is forbidden to be that which it naturally is.

It is the *taming* of the wildman that has turned him into a madman. So after hundreds of years of trying to calm the masculine, to tame and contain it, all to no avail, I propose a radical idea.

Let us be who we truly are.

What does this mean? Since we are so used to denying who we are, how do we bring real MEANING to the unfolding of our lives? The male is one of the two poles of the physical universe. Within our psyches lies the archetypes of the eagle, the warrior, the sky-walker and the wise man. Let us begin to own the positive aspects of these archetypes. To do this, we men must move beyond our shallow ego images of who we are, who we want to be and who we are afraid we are. We must learn to listen to and value our inner guidance. We must quiet our minds and learn to honor the earth. Our sisters can help us with this but, ultimately, we men must venture to our primal maleness with our brothers. We must learn to trust each other and ourselves. Only then will we be able to channel our wonderful, passionate, alive sense of deep, natural maleness into the role of true peacemaker, the Warrior of the Heart.

The FEMALE Journey to Wholeness

The path to wholeness for today's woman is leading her away from the surface role of powerless playmate (Personality Woman) and towards the self-reliant do-ing aspect of the YANG nature that lives inside of every woman. This integration of her outwardly creative power and will allows her to unlock an even deeper power, her Soft Power or Natural Woman Power.

When a woman embraces her YANG side, it's easy for her to get hooked on it and to become caught in the "Personality Man" outer world of competition and surface success. Women have been treated like second-class citizens in this outer world for so long that the temptation is there to "out-man the men." But this keeps her locked at the same level of game-playing that Personality Man is trapped.

Beneath and beyond the level of "integration of opposites" lies the wisdom and *real* power of women's natural heritage - a thread of ancient energy that has been passed to each woman by generations and generations of woman-spirit. Our planet aches for women to reconnect with and to live this kind of woman-warrior power.

This deep journey to a women's source of true power cannot be written about by a man. Only one who has the courage to claim her primal connection to that thread of *womanpower* that weaves its way back through the centuries has the right to write about this. I have asked a respected friend, Diana Long, a woman who has looked into the darkness and seen beyond it, to share with us. She writes...

I experience this journey of wholeness as, more than a passage into the unknown, an embracing, an encompassing, an integration of Mystery.

I have had many ideas in my life about what it means to be a "whole" woman. As I have stumbled through the process of assuming and discarding roles and personas, I have become acutely aware of my beliefs about my own "positive" and "negative" inner feminine and masculine. As I dealt with understanding the dynamics of my marriage of fourteen years, I unveiled many of the dynamics of my "inner marriage," that much desired integration of yin and yang within. At the deepest level of my unconscious I discovered that I did not trust either my inner feminine or masculine. As my awareness of the depth of my distrust of my self grew, my despair at not having any idea of how to authentically "Be" peaked, with the natural consequence of the shattering of my concepts of how to Be in relationship, and I fell into a seemingly bottomless abyss of grief and

despair. As I now continually surrender any precon-
ceptions of how to Be or how to love, I feel I am falling
ever deeper into that abyss, living in a space of woman-
power that I can only describe as Mystery. I am now in
the process of continually inviting and experiencing all
aspects of my self, yin and yang, to emerge and be acknowledged without labeling or judging. I feel as though
I am in the process of an "inner marriage." To the extent
that I cease to view others as objects of my own
unintegrated aspects, I am able to enter into an awesome dance of Mystery with them, allowing each of us
to continually discover and reveal ourselves to ourselves and to each other. This "inner marriage" is not
androgeny as I understand it, it is much deeper.

This is my "womans" journey now, my current dance.

I used to believe that I knew how to love, now I only
believe in Mystery. I know that I don't know how to love,
but I'm learning to fall into Mystery.

EXPLORING THE NATURAL WOMAN/NATURAL MAN
(Danaan's Workshop in Dublin, Ireland)

*There were nineteen of us in the workshop, ten women
and nine men. We were instructed to separate by sex and
choose a corner of the hall where we would create a
"ritual and symbol of meaning" for ourselves, a statement
of our connection. We men gathered in the far north
corner and immediately crouched down close to one
another to plan our ritual. Every so often we would glance
at the women, huddled together in their far south corner,
busy at their work of planning.*

*None of us really understood what we were to do. After
a while, it became clear that it didn't matter - WE were the
ritual and the symbol and whatever we created together
was exactly right.*

*When all was done and the women acted out their ritual
for us and we acted out ours for them, I knew we were
acting out some ancient, perhaps primal dance of woman
and man. The intricate details didn't seem to matter but
the energy flow was all important.*

The women, dancing their ritual, formed a tight circle, facing in towards the center. In the middle, they had assembled ornaments, food and precious things, and their dance carried them in and out from this center. They twirled and soared but always their circle was "energy-intact" and always their focus returned to the center and to the circle itself. They were like one being.

The women's bodies were the symbol. The maintenance of the circle was the ritual and the center was the reservoir of the energy. That reservoir swelled with power until finally the women collapsed, ecstatic, together on the floor. And still the circle remained intact.

After a long time, we men formed our circle, pressed close in a tight bond around our previously constructed center symbol. It was almost the exact same center symbol as the women had created. We began making deep-gut sounds; we swayed and twisted, we crawled in and out and on top of one another. We reformed our circle, rubbing hip to hip, and then ran screeching, outward to the far corners of the hall, flying, falling, jumping. Again and again, we ran back to our symbolic center, arriving and departing alone. Finally, we all gathered in a circle and stood, arm on shoulder, in silence. I remember the wonderful smell of sweat.

As I recall that wonderful ritual dance that spontaneously created itself at my workshop in Ireland, I absolutely know that what I have been talking about in this chapter is true.

There *are* deeper levels of positive, and perhaps ancient, power in us and much of it flows through the male and female bodies we now inhabit. These delightfully passionate and wise energies have been layered over by decades, maybe centuries of control, fear and "allowed behaviors" but they are still alive down there.

That pulsing circle of Irish women felt it in their ritual and so did the men. In their dances, the women oscillated from their circle to the center, circle to center, over and over again. The men oscillated from their circle outward and then back to the circle, over and over again. The circles survived and maintained their integrity. No concretized conclusions are needed, only the awareness of a powerful and natural force that flows through us; a force that each of us can reconnect with for the good of the whole.

When women and men have tapped this rich force of natural woman-power and man-power, they are free to express that force in their own unique, natural way. The point is that the outward physical expression of that force, no matter what one's sexual preference, will come from a deep, grounded, natural part of us, rather than the surface, reactionary, societal role.

Co-Creation

There is a knowing in me that we are rapidly approaching a time when there will be enough women on the planet who have re-connected with their Natural Woman and enough men who have re-connected with their Natural Man, that a new model of woman-man interaction will start to form in our collective unconscious. What will this new model look like? Be careful, don't drag out all your old pictures and fantasies and unfulfilled dreams based on your "Tonal," your "yesterday" view of the same old consentual reality.

The *new* model of man-woman relationships must come from the Nagual, not the Tonal (see pages 4 & 5). It's *your* job to find it as a Warrior of the Heart. Remember, the new warrior doesn't sit in the middle of the Tonal fantasizing and waxing eloquently about "how great it's gonna' be." The Warrior ventures out into the Nagual, the place between the trapezes, the Unknown, and opens herself or himself to Newness and brings it back to the tribe.

My intuition tells me that our new model of man-woman relationships (and also man-man and woman-woman interaction) will look *very* different from what we now expect. I know that whatever it looks like, the coming together of Natural Woman and Natural Man will unlock a co-creative force within our reality that will give birth to an incredible acceleration of personal and collective evolution. I can hardly wait.

In my article for *In Context* magazine titled "We're Not Ready Yet, But Soon," I tried to express my feelings about my own journey to my natural self through an event that happened on a strip of Pacific shoreline at the equinox with a group of men and women I love very much. In this Equinox ritual, the men and the women had separated to spend the night in their same-sex group to explore "natural man" and "natural woman".

"We're Not Ready Yet, But Soon"

I can see Andy through the fire. He's hopping from one foot to the other in some rhythmic way, to some perhaps ancient beat inside of him. The flames from our men's driftwood campfire leap thirty feet in the air and I am starting to feel that feeling again. It's the one that I feel every time I huddle around a campfire and I get very hot on one side of my body and very cold on the other side. Suddenly, I am no longer in this time, this place. I am somewhere in some ancient place and I am naked and my muscles and tendons resonate to some primal energy and I am man at the awakening of...I don't know what. I lose it at that point as though I am not supposed to remember. Not yet!

So here we are, Andy and me and Bob and a half dozen other men. It is spring equinox and we have come together to spend the night on this beach. Another group, all women, have chosen to spend the night on the mountain ridge. Separately, we will evoke the energies of our gender; we will try to open to our own, brothers to brothers, sisters to sisters, beyond role and game and expectation. We will try. We will use ritual and dance and story and whatever we can to explore who is this being, man; who is this being, woman. We have talked of what to do in the morning. An agreement - we, the men, will come to a meadow between the ocean shore and the mountain ridge. The women, too, will come there. We will meet and see what happens. We will try.

But now it's midnight, or one, or two in the morning, and my brothers and I are hot on one side and cold on the other. I am me and not me; I am very new and very old and, through it all, I know that I am man. It feels so incredibly good, incredibly right, to be here with these men in this way.

Later, the poet Robert Bly would give me a framework for these feelings as he re-introduces me to the masculine archetype of the "wildman" ("What Men Really Want," *New Age Journal*, May, 1982). This aspect of the male being is a deep, subconscious source of primary energy which, Bly contends, has been ignored by men in our desire to integrate the softer, more intuitive feminine aspects into our personas. The hostile behaviors of most present male cultural stereotypes are in sore need of balancing. This can be done and, in many ways, is being done by men who are allowing themselves to feel the soft, feminine aspects within them. The men on this beach this night have all been to this softer place and it is time to go deeper.

For now though, there is only the heat of the fire and my brothers and it is enough. I am full as I have not been full for a very, very long time.

The sun shows its first glow over the ridge and Andy is pulling me towards the water's edge. Now we are naked and running through the ocean surf and screaming. God, I love to scream. I mean REALLY scream. I'm freezing. The March Pacific ocean laps against my genitals and the morning sun paints its way over the ridge, across the lagoon and spills over my trembling body. From my belly button up, I am golden and warm; from there down, I am sea-green and cold. That ancient feeling is with me again.

From somewhere in me, from a place so deep I had not known it existed in me, there comes forth another scream. Not from my throat, my voice, my lungs, but from my belly, from some dark deep cave in the bowels of me. The scream explodes from me, an orgasm of emotion. You may have heard it! It was that loud, that powerful. My brothers stood frozen, drinking me in. Then, their screams echoed mine as we bathed the beach in joy. We FROL-ICKED. Have you ever seen grown men FROLIC? I thought my heart would burst.

Then the awareness of what had happened sank into me. There, in the freezing water, for the first moment in my life, I felt MAN and felt no guilt for it. Yes, for all my life, at some level just below my conscious awareness, I had felt guilty about being a man. Why? Perhaps because of some images of men as the "violent ones," the destroyers, the war-makers. I don't know; all I know is that it had been there, this low-grade chronic inability to fully embrace who I am. Now it was gone. Purged. Released.

*The molten, churning powerhouse of primal energy
that lies within my maleness is neither good nor evil - it is
simply pure energy. My consciousness is the force that
decides how this vast store of primal energy is used.
Because I and so many of my brothers are growing in
consciousness, we are beginning to honor the powerful
inner broadsword of creative action that is our way of
manifesting Light in physical form.*

*For the first time all night, we brothers shared words as
we excitedly talked of our fear and guilt and confusion. Of
the relationships that were "supposed" to bring us happiness, the success that was promised to bring us fulfillment.
Now we, here, were committing ourselves, our man-
selves, to use our strength, our will, our power to create
not destroy, to love not fear, to contribute what only man-
energy can contribute to the creation of a peace-filled
future for our world.*

*We are do-ers and we are learning to direct our do-ing
energy in ways of service and wholeness. Gandhi, Martin
Luther King and Anwar Sadat are glowing examples of
men who have owned their inner broadsword, their
positive do-ing nature.*

*It was time to go to the meadow. The women would be
there. Perhaps some clarity about the next step would be
there. In our circle before we left the beach, we shared
how hard it was to leave, to let go of this togetherness-
beyond-ego. But we also shared how important it is to
keep our commitments. So we walked together towards
the meadow.*

*We could see the women coming down the trail from
the mountain. Images of warm hugs and soft smells were
with me now. But as we approached the women, I noticed
that my body was beginning to close, just a bit. My
shoulders were hunching forward, just a bit. My freely
swinging hips were becoming just a bit more controlled,
more proper. Others noticed their body responses, too.
We were returning.*

*Then we were together, men and women, people who
care deeply for each other. We were looking at each other,
saying nothing. For a long time we just stood there facing
each other. One of the women broke the difficult silence.*

She said, "Not yet."
We all knew what she meant. We turned and walked
away. No more words were spoken for many hours.
Feelings of sadness and rightness swept through me. We
had touched something during that night, something so
deep and vital for me, man, and she, woman, that to
attempt to come together at that level *would have been*
impossible. For now.

There will come a time when men and women *will* come
together at that level. But first men, as men, and women, as
women, must explore the depths, the incredible depths of who
they are. They/we must risk and open and explore and claim
the woman-power and the man-power that live in that cave
deep within and yet beyond ourselves. We have only just
begun.

When we men and women have done that work and then
come together, the co-creation from that union will move us
from where we are to where we were meant to be.

Being a man, wanting to understand myself and also help
women understand who we are as men, I ask myself, "What is
this MAN-power, this deeper manifestation of who-I-am-as-
man?" The words that come to me are CREATE, RISK, EX-
PLORE, CHALLENGE, THRUST, GO BEYOND...and more - all
having that old, old feeling in me that I have come to associate,
in my societal experience with "getting in trouble." Hmmmmm.

THE TROUBLE WITH MEN...I'm walking along a beach,
just relaxing and enjoying the day. No one around except
the sea gulls and maybe a harbor seal. My car is up on the
road and so I begin the ascent to the top of the cliff, up the
gradual, nicely laid-out State Park trail. But then my eye
catches a glimpse of some interesting rocks to my left. I'll
bet I could make it up that way. It's steep, no trail, loose
rocks. What if I fell? Why take the chance? But in me there
is no question. My pants get filthy, my hands get cut, it's an
hour longer and I love it. What's that all about? Why didn't
I just stay on the nice trail?

I'm driving a motorcycle along the coast highway. The
bike is humming, every one of the hundreds of little parts
performing just right, to create a harmony, and I as driver
am a part of the harmony. At the same moment, I am in

charge of this assemblage and only a part of it, a piece of the whole. Is this just macho bullshit, or do I really experience a living connection to all of this? I feel a balance of me and us; me and the machine and the US that emerges from all of the parts working just right.

There's a curve coming up. I can see the road far ahead of it. If I take the curve at this speed there's a risk. Five miles an hour faster and I know I'll lose it. Five miles an hour slower asks nothing of me, of us. So what, there's nobody around to prove anything to. But I know already, beyond questions, beyond analysis, what I will do. I begin to feel that old body response to my adrenal glands doing their job. I can feel my parasympathetic nervous system flipping to ALERT, to "on-line, everybody...all hands on deck." My biocomputer shifts to high speed data analysis: "probability of patch of gravel around curve...probability of error in judgment about clear road ahead...awareness of amount of tread on tire...." My vision clears, focuses, soft eyes to take in the big picture, muscles alert and relaxed at the same time. We're going in. Not me, we. Every cell in me, every gene, every bolt and piston and spoke.

The curve is behind us now. WE goes back to ME and me develops a cold sweat and I can feel my left brain start to ask questions and make judgments: "You ass, you hot dog, you macho jerk. Why do you do those dumb things?"

Maybe because it's one of the very few ways that my culture allows me, that I allow me, to give life to an ancient need.

You see, it is our nature to feel and to desire the experience of intensity, of living at the edge, of challenge and risk-taking. That is not all we are but it is a natural, deep, wonderful part of who we are. This is the "inner fire" that infuses our actions with aliveness.

I have talked to so many Vietnam vets, my brothers who have experienced kill and/or be killed. They, most of them, ache. They are lost. They whisper to me of a terrible awareness that for the first time in their lives, on the battlefield facing probable death, they felt fully alive. Every experience since then has had a meaningless mediocre taste to it. How are we to make sense of all this? We MUST!

We cannot simplistically demand that humans stop hurting each other and think it will work. It's so much deeper than that. Do you think that there have not been "peace movements" for thousands of years? Do you think that women have not been begging and demanding men for thousands of years to evolve beyond their dominating, oppressive, violent behavior? Do you think that simply beating our swords into plowshares will change anything? What will we do with all those plowshares?

There is an intensity to us humans. It has something to do with pushing limits, with trying the untryable, with risking what is for what could be. It has caused a lot of trouble. This intensity has manifested in ways that pit us against one another, that inflate or deflate our personal egos and that objectify whatever or whomever gets in our way. So what to do?

In recent years, we have tried to one degree or another to let go of macho male and manipulative female ways of expressing our needs. After some difficult/wonderful years of exploring our yin and yang, we are beginning to hear the soft wisdom of our inner voice, our intuitive self. It whispers to us that our next journey in awareness is not towards androgyny, rather to deeper levels of maleness and femaleness. To explore that creative, passionate risker, that limit-pusher that burns to live 100%, beyond macho or victim, beyond any need to prove his or her worth.

We must never "cork the volcano" of our intensity. (Corked volcanoes explode.) We must develop the clarity and the self-love to direct its awesome power for good. Our world cries out for men and women to move beyond their role-playing and beyond their guilt and to unlock that deep, fertile naturalness that lives in us. Humankind hungers for good, grounded male energy, just as surely as it hungers for clear, deep, powerful woman energy. The integration of those creative forces will birth something very new, very wonderful.

NOT YET, BUT SOON!

I began this section with the idea that one of the "source conflicts" in our world is the misunderstanding, mistrust and hostility that exists between men and men, women and women, and women and men, and that we need to find out who we are beneath the superficial games we play within these roles.

Here I am suggesting that one of the "source resolutions" to the conflict in the world, one of the most effective tools we possess for *real* peacemaking, is *also* within the definition of *woman* and *man*. Of course, it demands that we throw out the old, dysfunctional definitions and claim the ancient/brand-new energies of who you are as a man or woman behind the dysfunction. Then you are ready for a *real* relationship.

TAKE YOUR NEXT STEP

Consider joining a men's group/women's group, one that is willing to explore the deeper levels of who-you-are and not just stay at the level of blaming of the other sex. This does *not* mean that you should not examine and express your anger and frustration at being taught and required to live a surface role for so many years. It just suggests that you use your anger to move you forward to the next step, which might be the exploration of that powerful, clear woman or man within you who can help your entire sex to release their need to stay "safe" at the level of personality woman or man and join you on the journey off the Tonal and out into the Nagual.

Chapter 21

Relationship as a Warrior Path

Egos Arousing
Spontaneous Combustion
Mis-Taken For Love
                                    Pat

"...the most pernicious myth about love is the image of
love as a closed system between two people or three
people, or one man and his country, his religion, his
race, his family. The sweet intimacy of love inevitably
turns rancid when it circles in upon itself and is not
open to the world. For love is a prism through which
one loves the whole world. Every intimacy and every
sweetness of love makes the whole world different and
opens one up to the world's reality rather than
protecting one from it."
                                    Al Carmines

One of the teaching stories from the Vedas of ancient India
is about Paravati's Fire. Paravati's Fire is the holy fire that
burns away the outer layers of wheat chaff exposing the kernel
of grain within. It is, metaphorically, the fire that burns away
our surface coverings and personas and veils of illusion so that
that we can access our inner core, our jewel at the center of the
lotus.

The Vedas say that if you want to stand close to Paravati's
Fire and burn away the chaff then you must do two things. "Do
not go to the mountaintop to meditate," the Vedas say, rather
"get involved in a relationship and go to the marketplace."

Ha! What great wisdom! Paravati's Fire doesn't exist up on
the mountaintop. We go there to still ourselves and to heal and
listen. The Fire, the one that's hot enough to roast away our
tough outer layers of chaff, burns right in the midst of relationship and in the heat of the marketplace. You know what I'm
talking about. In fact, I'll bet you thought you'd burn to death
a time or two in those environments. I have. But we don't, we

survive and hopefully we're a few layers of chaff closer to our core, our essence, our SELF because of it.

Warriors-in-Relationship

Let's face it, it is Relationship that forces us to look at how real our beliefs are, how much integrity exists in that which we profess to practice. *Real* relationship requires that we either "walk our talk" or shut-up. It can be our most demanding teacher.

You and I can use the vehicle of Relationship to accelerate our journey on our Warrior Path. If we are willing to stop settling for mediocrity in our lives, if we are willing to walk our talk about living a life of Integrity and Aliveness, then our relationships will give us just what we need to "check ourselves out." They will help us to make course corrections and to live in-between the trapezes.

All of our relationships can do this for the Warrior of the Heart; whether it is our relationships with our lovers, our parents, our children, our friends. Perhaps the clearest and most useful relationship-as-a-Warrior-Path is the one with your lover, your spouse, your "significant other." The ongoing, ever-changing dance of yin and yang with that person can be an opportunity for unparalleled growth, and where Paravati's Fire can burn its brightest and its hottest.

Exercise
WHEN WARRIORS MEET

I ask that you now recall your experience of your Warrior in the Meadow in the chapter on Aloneness. Whether or not it is the time for you to draw to yourself another Heart Warrior to be your teacher and student in the dance of intimacy and sexuality around Paravati's Fire, do this exercise anyway to help yourself to bubble to the surface and clarify these issues in your life.

Go back now to the drawing you did of yourself on page 47. Remember your symbols and garments, your shield and animals. *BE* that Warrior in the Meadow once again. Feel the presence of nature and feel your Warrior-self as an integral part of it all. You belong here in this beautiful place in nature.

Now look out across the meadow. Survey your surroundings. Drink in every aspect of your environment. Nothing escapes your awareness. There is movement on the far side of the meadow. A few deer and other wild animals wander across your view and you and they acknowledge each other with respect. But another energy attracts your attention, one that awakens dim and familiar *memories.*

Suddenly, with a prowess and centeredness that matches your own, another being emerges from the trees at the far corner of the meadow and now stands in the open. You experience many feelings at once - challenge, a tinge of fear, a sense of wonder, excitement. Who is this being who shows him/herself, not darting from tree to tree, but out in the open?

You move closer to study his/her garments. This person wears garments deliberately, consciously. His/her colors and design obviously signify his/her heritage and culture just as yours do. But the colors and their combinations, the fabrics and designs are very different from your own. What do they mean? What story do they tell? Are they a warning to you; is there danger here? Is this person a threat to you? Should you, as a Warrior, defend yourself?

But you are the *new* Warrior and your job is to venture into the Nagual to explore newness. You live between the trapezes and at this moment it feels like this meadow *is* the Nagual and you are right where you belong.

This other person has moved closer to you, studies you now. You notice that she/he moves from her/his center, grounded, connected to the earth. You are in the presence of a Warrior of the Heart.

Now you stand face to face. This person is in touch with her/his power. She/he does not demand that you be less than powerful. In fact, you feel an invitation to play, to match her/his power with your own, to explore the far boundaries of the possible with this person. You intuitively know that you are in "trouble." It is the kind of trouble that Zorba the Greek was talking about.

*Remember that wonderful old movie "Zorba the Greek?"
Remember the scene where the very proper young British
gentleman is shocked about something "unconventional"
(the Nagual) that Zorba has done? He says, "Zorba, you
can't do that; you'll get in trouble!" Zorba pulls himself up,
stares into the proper gentleman's eyes and declares,
"...trouble? Life is trouble! Only death is nice. To live is to
roll up your sleeves and embrace trouble."*

Out in that meadow, owning fully your connection to
your human heritage, your awareness of your natural
man or natural woman and also your Warrior-newness
and potential, you have drawn to you another Warrior.
This Warrior will call you to own your Integrity, your
Passion and your Aliveness. He or she will rip your little
pinkies off that old, worn-out trapeze bar you've been
hanging on to for so long. Yup, you are definitely in
trouble. That kind of trouble is where the Warrior of the
Heart belongs. Another word for this kind of trouble is
Intensity.

When Warriors meet, there are usually three types of emotional responses within them. One of them is *excitement.*
Finally, you have encountered someone to match power with
- the good, grounded, life-affirming power of "Hara"-connected-
to-heart. No games needed here, no throttling back, no hours
of explanation, no compromise. You sense the possibility of
win-win, of 1 + 1 = 3, of living 100% with no apologies and you
are *excited.*

Another emotion is *fear.* It's as if that part of you that has not
fully embraced your Heart Warrior Path knows that its time is
short, its number's called, its clinging to old trapezes is about
to become history. There is nowhere left to hide and the old
games won't work with this person. That old, dysfunctional
part of your ego is going to have to die and it's not going to die
gracefully. It will kick and scream and cajole and use every
dirty, manipulative trick you have ever learned to stay alive. It
won't work but it will probably raise hell with your life before
it lets go. See what I mean about *trouble?* Welcome it. Celebrate
it.

It is the signal, the herald of true change in your life. You are
moving forward towards a level of integrity and clarity and
right-ness that you have never experienced before. Whatever

it takes – it's worth it.

The other emotional response, the final one, is a different kind of feeling and difficult to describe unless you have already felt it. The best word for it is *Knowing*. Here you are, standing face to face with this other Warrior of the Heart. She/he is very different, perhaps even strange; an end-point of a thread of Warrior-lineage that weaves its way back in time through different, perhaps totally foreign beliefs and symbols and "truths." You feel excitement and fear yet, at the same time, you are completely calm. You have never been more calm or centered or fully in touch with every faculty in your body/mind in your entire life.

You *know*. Know what? That's an irrelevant question. That's an old, bullshit question from the old trapeze, from the Tonal. You just *know*. (I told you it's difficult to describe it unless you've already experienced it.) It just feels *right*, it all makes sense, it all shakes into place. The experience is something like, "Oh, of course, this is *exactly* where I belong (even though your logical brain may be screaming at you to get the hell out of there)."

I have experienced this sense of *rightness* a few times in my life. I felt it with Mother Teresa. I felt it in Belfast after my experience with the mother, her baby and the British soldiers. I feel it with a few of my male friends with whom I give myself permission to explore the meadows and caves of our *Natural Man*. I feel it with a few of my sisters who are on their journey of discovery of their *Natural Woman*. And, I *always* feel it with the dolphins.

There have been a few times when a woman and I have been standing in that meadow. We have worn our garments proudly and consciously. We have acknowledged the power of the other, acknowledged the excitement and the fear. We have felt the knowing. We danced in that meadow, first tentatively, each dancing his and her own dance, filled with the movements, sounds and rituals of our uniqueness. Then slowly, never breaking eye contact, never losing our centers, we have blended. *Ki*, life-force, flowing in *Ai*, harmony, on a shared *Do*, path of upward, spiral motion. Paravati's fire. I have done the dance of yang and yin with a Woman Warrior of the Heart and it has brought my Man Warrior of the Heart deeper and closer to its blending with my Natural Man. It has helped me to remember the incredible mystery that my life is. And, it has been trouble, *Zorba trouble*.

Exercise
YOUR PARTNER AS WARRIOR

Remember your drawing of your own Warrior of the Heart. I suggest that you give a try at also drawing your lover in her/his Warrior garb on the drawing on the next page. But first, here's a suggestion:

A. Make two copies of the page *before* you do a sketch of your relationship partner in his or her Warrior garb. Then go ahead and do the sketch in this book as you imagine him/her to be when in touch with their Heart Warrior nature (even if you've never seen them be in touch with it, in your opinion). Then, give the two blank copies to your partner and ask if he/she would be willing to sketch him/herself and also to sketch you as a warrior. You'll need to explain the process to your partner.

Or

B. Buy a copy of this book for your partner so he/she can read about the conceptual framework in all the previous sections and do his/her sketches with the same background that you now have.

Whether you choose A. or B., the whole idea, of course, is to have you and your partner sit down and share all four drawings when they are done. Make sure that you give yourselves enough time and have co-created a safe-space within which the sharing takes place. Then *listen* to each other, respectfully and with the sense of wonder that comes from being in the presence of a fellow Warrior who is sharing gifts from the Nagual.

A word of caution: Don't make a religion out of this, please. Just because someone's partner does not resonate with this particular concept of Warrior of the Heart or just because she/he doesn't want to do this (or any other) exercise with you does not mean that they are not the partner for you. Don't put people in boxes! There are lots of Heart Warriors out there who simply use other definitions, images and metaphors to describe themselves.

NOTE: if you are not now in relationship, consider using the following sketch to draw your image of that other person with whom you would *like* to "dance in the meadow."

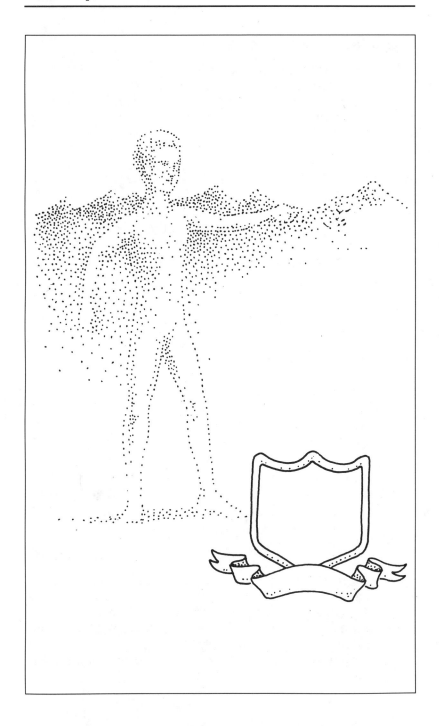

Upgrading our Relationships

In my own life, I have been painfully aware of how difficult it is to live as a Warrior, in any sustained way, for more than brief periods of time. That old daily grind comes in and I seem to let my Warrior garments become shabby and threadbare. I take on the mantle of mediocrity that my culture says is the "way it is" and I *compromise*.

That word *compromise* gets used a lot these days. "We have to learn to compromise," it is said. Bullshit. Compromise is what we all have been doing for centuries and it is a no-win setup. Webster's dictionary defines *Compromise* as: "a settlement in which each side gives up some demands or makes concessions." The next definition of it in Webster's says: "a laying open to danger, suspicion or disrepute." I think the latter should be the *first* definition, especially in relationships.

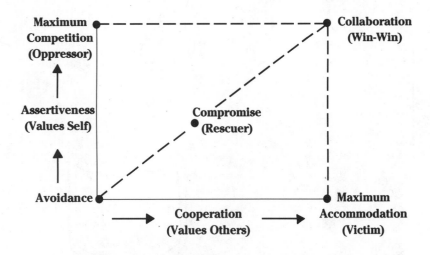

In my work in conflict resolution, I frequently make us of this simple chart. I wish I would use it more in my own relationships. This chart helps us to identify our balance between our cooperation with others and our assertiveness about opur own wants and needs. Another way I like to see it is that it helps us identify how much we value others and how much we value ourselves.

Notice the point on the chart labeled "avoidance". A person whose behavior is located at this point is simply not willing to assert him/herself, to value him/herself, nor are they willing to cooperate with others. Persons who are at the point labeled "victim" are exhibiting behavior that gives away their power. They are quite willing to cooperate with others, but are unwilling to assert themselves. They refuse to stand up for themselves. The opposite pole to the victim is the "oppressor", where people assert themselves but refuse to cooperate with others. In other words, they are very willing to "say their own truth", but are unwilling to listen to anyone else's truth.

The point labeled "compromise" is an interesting one. Compromise happens when we assert ourselves "a little" and cooperate with others "a little". It's called "let's be fair". Until recently, most literature taught that "compromise" was a good place to go for. After all, they said, you've got to give a little to get a little, right? So you compromised, and your head said "Well, it's the best I could get" and your guts said "How come I feel so awful, like I just sold my integrity down the drain?" It seems that compromise just doesn't work very well, certainly not over time. Everybody winds up feeling like they didn't *really* get what they wanted.

To truly create a space of "win-win", where everyone feels honored and affirmed we must go all the way to "collaboration". This requires us to "give 100%", to be willing to be fully assertive, fully valuing ourselves, and also to be fully cooperative, facilitating the others to reach their full value. This means not "settling", not avoiding the conflict. It means coming back over and over again, and getting to the source conflicts underlying the presenting problem. Only when the source conflicts are squarely addressed can we collaborate an "all-win" solution.

If we don't value others or ourself, then there is zero cooperation and zero assertiveness (avoidance). When we cooperate with others but don't value our own wants and needs, we fall into accommodation or the *victim* role. If we *only* value our own wants and needs and don't give a damn about the wants and needs of others, we end up with pure "get 'em before they get you" competition or the *oppressor* role.

Look at the place *compromise* occupies on the chart. It sits at the intersection of "some" cooperation and "some" assertiveness. In other words, everybody gets some of what they want and, almost invariably, everyone goes away feeling a little cheated. Everyone feels like they have given away their integrity to "keep the peace" (that's the old definition of peace). That is definitely *not* win-win. But it is a lot easier; it doesn't require you to give and live 100%.

Compromise is a way to avoid conflict. It's a method for settling for less than 100% and for hanging on to your *position*. It *rescues* you from really becoming intimate with others.

Let's talk about rescuers, victims and oppressors. If you have studied transactional psychology, you have probably encountered the O-R-V triangle as discussed previously. Here it is:

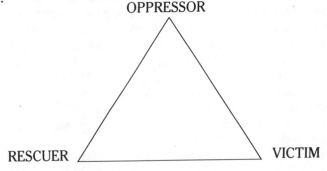

This "relationship triangle" represents the three roles we get stuck in, in a dysfunctional relationship. At any particular time in the unfolding drama of your relationship, you might find yourself playing out the role of *oppressor*, the dominating bad guy who has all the power (but not really) and uses it to oppress his/her partner. At another time, you might be the *victim*, the powerless (but not really) oppressed one who "gives in" to the bully. At another moment, you might become the *rescuer* who "saves the victim" (your partner or yourself - whoever is playing victim at that moment). The rescuer prevents the oppressor and the victim from really dealing with each other. The rescuer tries to keep things "nice" and "safe" (old definitions). The rescuer guarantees the no-win outcome of *compromise*.

There is another way to play this game. It's called *collabora-*

tion. Built into this collaboration is a powerful idea that can not only help to create the win-win situation, but it also can move you forward on your journey toward awakening from oppressor, victim or rescuer, all the way to Warrior of the Heart.

The dictionary defines "collaboration" as: "the art of working together." In the chart, you can see that collaboration requires both maximum assertiveness *and* maximum cooperation. In other words, it asks that you value yourself 100% and also that you value others 100%. How can this be? It *can* be because this reality of ours is *not* a closed system. It's an open system wherein I can give 100% to you and still have 100% to give to me.

Collaboration means that you work to make sure that *everybody wins*, not to settle for less. Collaboration means that you don't sell yourself short nor do you sell the other person short. You stick with it, you keep on communicating and exploring alternatives. You keep listening for the real *source conflicts* beneath the *presenting problems* because it is at the level of "resolution of source conflicts" that true *collaboration* occurs.

Compromise is problem solving at the level of *presenting problems* and that is why it feels like nobody got what they really wanted. Of course they didn't. Each of us intuitively knows that solutions to surface presenting problems is not what we really want. Even though we go through these elaborate cover-ups, each of us is praying inside that someone will care enough to rip off our bandages and see who we really are. I promise you that relationship, *real* relationship, will rip your bandages off. Or, maybe I should say *burn* them off. Remember Paravati's Fire?

I enjoy the fact that the second definition of *collaboration* given in Webster's, right after "working together," is: "to cooperate with the enemy." That's perfect. You'll know what I'm talking about when you read the section called Politics of the Heart.

Think about this phrase "cooperate with the enemy" in terms of your present love relationship. When I get to the point in my love relationship where I am drowning in mediocrity, where my Warrior spirit is nowhere to be found, I do tend to assign to my partner the role of enemy. (After all, it's her fault that I have compromised, right? I've settled for less to keep the peace and she damn well better be grateful. Oh, yeah?)

It's time for me to go for *collaboration*. It's time for Zorba the

Greek to get off his "washing machine and go over and sit next to the lady in the laundromat" who just happens to be my lover.

It's time to create a safe-space with my lover so we can explore just what 100% means to each of us. For each, it will mean different things and maybe some similar things as well. It's time to listen and to breathe. It's time to let go of my *position*, which keeps me chained to my *presenting problems*, so that *we* can cooperatively attack the *source conflicts* in our relationship. We need maximum assertiveness blending with maximum cooperation, maximum valuing of self and maximum valuing of our partner, no less. We need a deep conviction that I can have it all and so can you, and a commitment to get beyond the silly, hurting roles and games where only win-lose is possible and stay with it until we get to the clarity of what I *really* want and what she *really* wants. That's a place where win-win is possible. That's collaboration; that's cooperating with the "enemy."

When we reach *that* point of clarity, it is all too obvious that the only "enemy" is in our own dark shadow which we have projected out onto our lover, probably to keep ourselves separate and "safe" because intimacy is so scary. But at the point of *collaboration*, the Warrior of the Heart stands eye to eye with the Warrior of the Heart in the meadow, in between trapezes. Intimacy becomes a way of life.

Release

Perhaps the most difficult step in Relationship as a Warrior Path is when a person must admit that their present love relationship is an old trapeze. First of all, there are two pitfalls that demand absolute awareness. One is the "grass is always greener" pitfall. Yes, there are rare times when the old games and roles are so entrenched in a relationship, when the life in that relationship has been drowned by the mediocrity of it, that collaboration is not possible and one must release one's grasp of that old trapeze and move forward. But so often, "flight" is used as an excuse for not facing one's own shadow. Healing and upgrading our relationships is a task of every Warrior of the Heart (regardless of whether we stay or go).

If we do go, if "choosing life" means letting go of that old relationship, then a second pitfall is the seizing of another trapeze too soon. In our loneliness, in our need to heal and be comforted, so often we grab whatever new trapeze bar comes along or even create a new one before we have released the old one.

Remember that in-between state, out there in the Unknown. That is a powerful place of growth and change and it must be experienced fully if we are to really grow. Otherwise, we just keep grabbing the same old bar with a new paint job.

6
REACHING OUTWARD

"You may say I'm a dreamer but I'm not the only one."
John Lennon

Chapter 22

Politics of the Heart

This Wholeness, At-oneness
Openness In Letting Others In
Free Of My Slavery

John

It's time to get radical. When you look at the course of human history, what you see is little advances on the same old theme. You see small improvements in a virtually unchanged system of inter-relationship. When you care enough to peek beneath the sophistication and adaptation that has occurred in the last 1000 years, you see that most humans on the planet are still dealing with each other from the position of mistrust, scarcity and alienation that characterized the dark ages.

Let's look at *real* change. Let's have the guts to try something *really* new instead of bandages on a system of game-playing that shouldn't be fixed but allowed to die a natural death.

That something new is called Politics of the Heart. I choose to use the word *politics* because politics has to do with power and people and change. That's what a Warrior of the Heart has to work with, and to do it with integrity.

Here are the guidelines for Politics of the Heart:

1. Give away your secrets.

2. Invite the enemy into your camp.

3. Find out what your enemy needs and give it to him/her/ them.

4. Find out what you need and ask for it clearly from your enemy.

5. Find out what your planet needs.

I'm purposefully using this strong word *enemy* in these guidelines. Look under the ego-image of yourself and you'll probably see that you are holding *enemy energy* on at least one person, perhaps a whole group of people.

> **"It's fun to do the impossible."**
> **Walt Disney**

Sound crazy? Can you imagine governments doing it? I'll bet that a dozen arguments come to mind to support the notion that it won't work. Can you imagine *yourself* doing it? Maybe *two* dozen reasons come to you as to why it wouldn't happen. But I don't think that anyone has ever really tried it, so how do we know?

Well, how much of it *could* work? When you look at each of the five guidelines, just how far could you go in each of them?

To answer this, the first thing you'd have to do is:

1. Identify what your secrets are.

2. Identify who your "enemy" is.

3. Identify what your *camp* is (what are you protecting?).

4. Identify what you need (not specifically related to your enemy; what do you need to feel better in general?).

5. Ask the "enemy" what he/she/they need.

6. Think about the greater need; what's best for the whole.

All this needs to be accomplished before any actualization of any of the guidelines is set in motion. Even if you never got beyond this step, you will have created some wonderful awareness in your life. You also may then discover that actualizing some of the guidelines will be be easier and safer than you thought.

Also every time you think about changing something, even if it's simply the "positions" that you and someone else hold about each other, ask yourself the question: How does this affect the whole, the larger family, the earth itself? Are the needs of the whole served, as well as my/our personal needs?

I choose to use the word planet here to draw awareness to the typically unconsidered needs of our "home" which is itself a living, conscious being co-evolving with the living creatures on its surface. Imagine bringing in this dimension of "planetary good" every time you make a decision. You may find that many times the answer to this larger inquiry is "the whole is not affected by this particular decision." But you will have acknowledged the whole, nonetheless, and that's the win/win consciousness.

Exercise : YOUR Politics of the Heart

CREATING REAL CHANGE IN YOUR LIFE

What the heck, let's give it a try, right now. Do it right in this book and then rip the page out and maybe paste it in your journal or diary or tape it to your bathroom mirror for a week.

1. What are my secrets (the ones I don't tell anyone)?

2. Who is my "enemy" (don't rationalize it away)?

3. Where's my camp?

4. What do *I* need?

5. What does my "enemy" need? (Write my intuitive hunch about what he/she/they need. I need to check this out with them.)

6. How does all of the above affect the greater good, the needs of the earth and all its creatures?

7. Okay, what's my next step with all this? (action step)

"And you have been told 'love your friends, hate your enemies.' But now I tell you: love your enemies and pray for those who persecute you..."

The words of Jesus,
from Matthew 5:43

Chapter 23

A Vision of Love

"Is there no vision of love to bind us together?"
John Denver

I feel so blessed to be working in a field that allows me to see the massive positive changes that are occurring on our planet. Not only am I in close networking contact with hundreds of groups doing hundreds of effective programs for global understanding but I also get to visit every corner of the globe. In *every* place I go there are large numbers of people who are working diligently and joyfully for a better world for us all. It *IS* happening. You won't read about most of it or see it on television because most media has not yet grown beyond the need for sensationalism and because the nature of this positive change process is necessarily "grassroots," close to the earth, word of mouth, done by "just folks" and not by big shots. Its great strength and resiliency is in its dispersed, decentralized structure. This global grassroots wave of positive change is a hologram, not a pyramid. A hologram is when every point is the center and the old pyramid power structures cannot destroy a new model of power where every person is the center.

From my hands-on experience of this global shift comes my Vision of Love. It is a practical, real life vision that is already beginning to happen. This is no pie-in-the-sky fantasy of a planet of white-robed light-beings coming to earth to rescue us and take us to that big hot tub in the sky. This is a vision of real people learning to experience their oneness through their differences.

My vision was born a few years ago on a rainy morning in Cherkassy, in the Ukraine, USSR. I had brought a group of American children to the Soviet Union to meet Russian, Georgian and Ukrainian children.

On this rainy morning, we were all out in the backyard of an elementary school in Cherkassy, near the Dneiper River that flows to the Black Sea. The Ukrainian kids and the American kids were planting a few trees together. The school teacher had arranged it to symbolize the bonding of our two cultures.

My attention was drawn to one team of diggers. It was 13-year old Rosie Cole from Bodega, California and Natasha, a 13-year old Ukrainian girl with blond hair down to her waist. They were digging this hole to plant a birch tree, a "beriozka," the Ukrainian symbol of peace. Rosie and Natasha were laughing and slipping in the mud, hanging on to each other and throwing dirt on each other's shoes and laughing some more. They were doing everything except digging that hole and it was delightful.

At one point, they both sank their shovels into the earth and came up with a shared lump of dirt, their shovels touching. As they raised that shared shovel full of earth together, they looked up and their eyes met. It was a moment when the world stopped.

I stood there watching in awe as their eye contact continued. Rosie and Natasha saw one another. And the world was healed. I imagined that in that moment, this child of America and this child of the USSR, were saying silently to one another, "I know you. You are my sister, not my enemy. And no one, no government, NO ONE will ever make me forget. We will find a way to heal this world - together."

You are Rosie. There is a Natasha out there who hasn't seen you yet, hasn't looked into your eyes so that both of your worlds can be healed. Maybe the name isn't Natasha, maybe it's Carlos or Abdul or Na-Dang.

GIVE YOUR GIFT

Do you know about the concept of the "trim-tab?" Well, on every ship there is a rudder, right? On large ships, it takes a very big rudder to make the ship go in the right direction. This big rudder requires a lot of power to move it - chains, pulleys, motors and servomechanisms. You alone couldn't budge that massive rudder without huge systems helping you to do it.

But, on every rudder of every large ship, there is a trim- tab. It's a small piece of metal attached to the rear of the rudder. It smooths out the fluctuations in the course of the ship and, without it set just right, the ship will wander back and forth, on and off its course. Because it's so small and because it is positioned in the right place on the rudder for maximum effect, it requires *very* little power to move it. You, one person, could do it all by yourself. You don't need to get large systems to do it for you.

Every one of us has a "trim-tab." Each of us has a gift to give which is our personal "trim-tab" to help our ship (Spaceship Earth) get "on course." You don't need to ask permission to use it. You don't need to get approval from "them" to use it. In fact, you are the only one who *can* use it and *we need you to start using it! Now!*

What is your trim-tab? Are you a masseuse? Use that gift to heal the world. Let go of "safe" and find a way to massage the pregnant belly of a woman in Leningrad. Go to West Virginia and rub the feet of an old black man and don't say, "I'm here to heal you;" rather say, "Let me sit at your feet, grandfather, and rub them as you teach me what I must learn."

Are you an accountant, graphics artist, computer operator or programmer? Get off your washing machine and go work with Amnesty International or Food First or a local drug-rehabilitation center or a mediation center or any of the many organizations in your area who are *doing* something. Help them to be more effective and more loving. Don't do it forever, just for a while. Go make a difference with the tools that you have and let it change you. Then, come back and do it where you were planted (in your neighborhood and family) and transform that, too. *Be* the Vision of Love. You do it by sharing what is right in front of you. It is the sharing, it is the courage to open your boundaries and invite others to open theirs that heals the world. It's the *means* that count, not the ends.

I'm always asked, "How?" "How can I do it? I don't even know how to get started." Stop asking that powerless, inhibiting question. Own your own power; change this Vision to make it *your* Vision of Love. Start telling people about your dream. Start looking for open doors, relevant organizations, leads. Start opening yourself to "trouble." The way will be shown when *you* show that you are serious about walking your talk.

My Vision of Love is a world full of people who simply share their gifts with each other. It is a vision of 10,000 people marching to Washington, DC, not to ask the government for lower taxes or demand more of something but to plant trees,

500,000 of them, to bring the lungs back to the choked inner city. As we tear up the concrete from an abandoned parking lot or old warehouse, we look up into the eyes of our fellow digger and they are the eyes of a Vietnamese Viet Cong veteran from Da Nang and the eyes of a Palestinian from Beirut and a young ghetto youth from DC itself. Our shovels clink together and we laugh and I throw dirt on your shoes. And we heal the world, together. I've already taken my first step towards my own vision of love. It's called PeaceTrees India, PeaceTrees Costa Rica and now Urban PeaceTrees USA.

Exercise

What is *your* Vision of Love? What is *your* trim tab? Write it now, before your head tears it apart and tells you twenty reasons why it won't work...

My Vision of Love is:

My Trim Tab is:

Urban PeaceTrees

Now here's a project that we can all get involved in. This is my next step in my "vision of Love." It is a step that I can do now with the tools that I have. It's my "Trim-tab" at work.

The Earthstewards Network through its PeaceTrees programs has brought together hundreds of young people from countries such as India, Costa Rica, Russia, the U.S.A., Northern Ireland, Japan, Nepal and Germany. They have helped reclaim desert in Southern India, replant the rainforests in Costa Rica, and revitalize our paved-over inner cities as well as reforest the Pacific Northwest in the U.S. They learned about each other's cultures, made friends, and returned home with new skills for living in our global community. As they worked together, they discovered how very much alike they are, how totally interdependent this planet of ours is, and how their new friendships are the hope of a better world for us all.

Projects like this are part of my vision of love. In this world of armed borders and broken families, you and I have the power to reach out and create a completely new model of what a functioning global community looks like. It starts here, with us. Through the Earthstewards Network, you and I have the chance to become a part of an active, vital global community, to become a part of a global network of people who know what it feels like to be a part of the positive process of change.

Through the Earthstewards Network, I hope to develop a healthy global family, working together to create a positive change. I invite you to join us.

PEACETREES

Did you know that you use up one large tree for every 120 pounds of paper you use? That is one tree for each 24 reams of 8½" x 11" 20# paper.

PeaceTrees is asking you to replenish the trees you use up in paper products. And you can do it in a way that supports and encourages youth to turn away from violence, learn leadership and team-building skills, and take pride in healing the earth.

It's easy! Photocopy and enlarge this tree diagram.

A) Record start date here: _____

B) Cross-out one tree-section each time you use:

   1. *one ream of paper*
   2. *two reams of pre-con-sumer recycled paper*
   3. *three reams of post-consumer recycled paper*
   4. *a large box of enve-lopes*
   5. *a case of paper towels (eight rolls)*
   6. *a case of toilet paper*

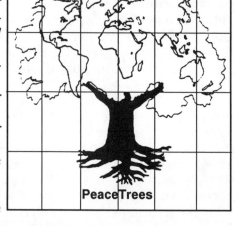

C) When you have used up a tree, record date here: _____
   How many weeks did it take for you to use up a tree? _____

D) Please send the above information to the Earthstewards Network with your tax-deductible donation of $10 (U.S. dollars) to replace the tree. Three dollars will be used to buy a sapling; seven dollars will help support a youth from a war-torn or ghetto community at a PeaceTrees site for three weeks.

E) Every three months, Earthstewards will calculate the num-ber of trees you use up per quarter and send to you a S.A.S.E. with a donation request for $10 per tree.
   You will receive a map of where your trees are planted, photos of the young men and women planting them, a handsome *"we replace our paper with PeaceTrees"* decal, and press release material to tell your community that you care about our planet and its kids.

Earthstewards Network
P.O. Box 10697, Bainbridge Island, WA 98110 (206) 842-7986

Chapter 24

Getting On With It...

"The thickness of your skin will be seven spans, for you will be proof against anger, offensive action, and criticism. With endless patience you shall carry out your duty, and your firmness shall be tempered with compassion for your people. Neither anger nor fear shall find lodgement in your mind, and all your words and actions will be tempered with calm deliberation. In all your official acts, self-interest shall be cast aside. You shall look and listen to the welfare of the whole people, and have always in view, not only the present but the coming generations — the unborn of the future Nation."

**Dekanawidah, to the
leaders of the
Iroquois Confederation**

So my friend, this book must end, not with my words, but with yours. I claim the right to call you friend because I have shared much of my life with you in these pages, sometimes embarrassingly. You now know me at close to the level that I know myself (maybe more in some areas because I'm too close to me to see). This shared journey we have taken must conclude with *your* words because only then will the journey have been your Warrior's journey.

Exercise

I ask you now to claim your power as you explore what all of this has meant to you in terms of your own path as a positive agent of conscious change on our beloved earth. Please take some valuable time now to write down your thoughts and feelings about:

Your PASSION. Tell yourself about your Passion...

Your TRAPEZE. What trapeze are you still clinging to for fear of letting go?

When do you feel "open?" What helps you to feel that way?

When do you feel powerful?

What do you do that you feel proud of? How can you do more of that? How can you do it so that the Earth is proud of you, too?

Go inside and identify the five elements in you that you know are your Warrior spirit...

1.

2.

3.

4.

5.

How can you manifest these Warrior elements more in your daily life?

What is your Commitment-of-Integrity as a Warrior of the Heart? (Don't think about it. Just write it down.)

Good journey, my sister or brother Warrior. I will meet you in some "laundromat of life" one day and we will know each other. Namaste.

Danaan Parry

ABOUT DANAAN PARRY

I met Danaan Parry in Reston, Virginia, at his three-day Warriors of the Heart workshop, in which he teaches conflict resolution and leadership skills. Recognizing him from a photo I'd seen, I watched him hug people when he arrived. Hugging Parry, I decided, must be like hugging a declawed grizzly bear. On closer inspection, I found that he has eyes so soft and inviting, you want to crawl into them for a nap. He has freckles all over his face and on the top of his bald head. Parry carries his bear body like that of a feline, probably as a result of twelve years' training in aikido. When he talks, his gestures are deliberate and his hearty laugh seems to leap out of its own accord.

"You can wrestle with your internal dragons or project them onto others," Parry tells workshop participants. He encourages them to be "warriors" in the Buddhist sense, which means those with the courage to know themselves (dark side included) and to face their own fears. For the Yaqui of northern Mexico, he observes, warriors are those who bring change to the tribe. Indeed, bringing about change in people's lives is the crux of Parry's work.

Parry grew up in Keansburg, New Jersey, "a funky little amusement park town," where he ran the ferris wheel as his summer job. With degrees from Rutgers and the University of California at Berkeley, he spent eight years in nuclear physics with the Atomic Energy Commission. He quit to pursue a degree in clinical psychology and worked as a therapist for a while before once again deciding he wanted a change. He travelled around the world, went to India and studied with a Native American shaman in Hawaii. During his shamanic training, he fell off a cliff and nearly died. It was a profound experience that led him into a year of isolation, after which he found a spiritual community in the redwoods of northern California.

After meeting Mother Teresa, Parry felt a need to "come out into the world again." He turned his desire for peace into active peacemaking by creating the Holyearth Foundation, through which he practices conflict resolution on a worldwide level. Groups he has worked with include Moslems and Christians in Pakistan, and Catholics and Protestants in Northern Ireland.

The Earthstewards Network is the branch of the Holyearth Foundation that brings together people in the United States and abroad "who support one another as they co-create a more peaceful, caring world." The Network sponsors many programs, including citizen diplomacy tours to such countries as Northern Ireland and the Soviet Union. One project involves sending youths from the United States, the Soviet Union and Third World countries to work camps in India and Costa Rica. The Network also offers Warriors of the Heart workshops in various locations, providing training that enables people "to transform the negativity in their lives into usable, positive action."

                                                              - **Dana Branscum**

© The Sun: A Magazine of Ideas, 107 North Roberson Street, Chapel Hill, North Carolina 27516 (Issue 151: June 1988)

READING LIST

(Books that have helped me on my journey)

Bach, Richard. *Illusions: Adventures of A Reluctant Messiah.*

Bateson, Gregory. *Steps To An Ecology Of Mind.*

Beer, Jennifer. *Peacemaking in Your Neighborhood: Reflections on an Experiment in Community Meditation.*

Brown, Lester. *State Of The World: A Worldwatch Institute Report on Progress Toward a Sustainable Society.*

Carlson, Don, and Craig Comstock, ed. *Citizen Summitry: Keeping The Peace When It Matters Too Much To Be Left To The Politicians.*

Casteneda, Carlos. *Journey To Ixtlan*

Crum, Thomas. *Magic of Conflict: Turning A Life of Work Into A Work Of Art.*

Eisler, Raine. *Chalice and The Blade: Our History, Our Future.*

Elgin, Duane. *Awakening Earth.*

Fields, Rick. *Chop Wood, Carry Water: A Guide To Finding Spiritual Fulfillment in Everyday Life.*

Fisher, Roger, and William Ury. *Getting To Yes: Negotiating Agreement Without Giving In.*

Fulghum, Robert. *All I Really Need To Know I Learned in Kindergarten: Uncommon Thoughts on Common Things.*

Harman, Willis. *Global Mind Change: The Promise of The Last Years of the Twentieth Century.*

Heider, John. *The Tao of Leadership: Lao Tzu's Tao Te Ching Adapted For A New Age.*

Juergensmeyer, Mark. *Fighting with Ghandi.*

Jung, Carl. *Memories, Dreams and Reflections.*

Larson, J. and M. Cyrus-Micheels. *Seeds Of Peace: A Catalog Of Quotations.*

Macy, Joanna. *Despair and Personal Power in The Nuclear Age.*

Marks, Linda. *Living With Vision: Reclaiming The Power Of The Heart.*

Millman, Dan. *The Way Of The Peaceful Warrior: A Book That Changes Lives.*

Mindell, Arnold. *The Leader as Martial Artist.*

Mindell, Arnold. *The Shaman's Body.*

Parry, Danaan, and Lila Forest. *The Earthsteward's Handbook.*

Peck, Scott. *The Different Drum: Community Making and Peace.*

Ram Dass, and P. Gorman. *How Can I Help? Stories & Reflections on Service.*

Schlindler, C. and P. Lapid. *The Great Turning: Personal Peace, Global Victory.*

Schmookler, Andrew. *Parable of The Tribes: The Problem of Power in Social Evolution.*

Starhawk. *Truth or Dare: Encounters With Power, Authority and Mystery.*

Swimme, Bryan. *The Universe is a Green Dragon: The Cosmic Creation Story.*

Theobald, Robert. *Rapids of Change: Social Entrepreneurship in Turbulent Times.*

Trungpa, C. *Shambhala: Sacred Path of the Warrior.*

Warner, Gail and Michael Shuman. *Citizen Diplomat: Pathfinders in Soviet American Relations.*

IMPORTANT REFERENCE MATERIALS

In Context — a Magazine of Humane, Sustainable Culture
P.O. Box 11470
Bainbridge Island, WA 98110

Surviving Together — a Chronicle of all US/USSR
Citizen Diplomacy
I.S.A.R.: a Clearinghouse on
Grassroots Cooperation in Eurasia
Suite 301
1601 Connecticut Ave. NW
Washington DC 20009

Utne Reader
LENS Publishing Co., Inc.
Suite 330
1624 Harmon Place
Minneapolis, MN 55403

Peace and Conflict Studies — list of college and
professional programs
Guide to Careers and Graduate Education in Peace Studies
Five College Program in
Peace & World Security Studies
c/o Hampshire College
Amherst, MA 01002

Journal of Conflict Resolution
Sage Publications, Inc.
2455 Teller Rd.
Thousand Oaks, CA 91320

Gesundheit by Patch Adams, M.D.
Healing Arts Press
1 Park St.
Rochester, VT 05767

"waRRIORs of the heaRt" workshops

The training of the peace professional . . .
with Danaan Parry

From time to time, Danaan leads weekend workshops around the United States and Europe. "Warriors of the Heart" training will give you skills for conflict resolution resulting in personal and planetary transformation.

Imagine knowing how to respond to mistrust, anger and hostility so as to transform them into energy.

The skills and awareness that I call on for my conflict-resolution work in "hot spots" on the planet are the same ones that you can use tomorrow, to transform negativity and fear into *aliveness*.

We have been conditioned to live at the 40% level, while our world, drowning in mediocrity, cries out for us to risk 100%, to live fully alive, and to be instruments of peace with every breath we take.

There is a new breed emerging, women and men who carry the essence of the peaceful warrior into their relationships, into their business, into every aspect of their lives. It makes their lives work, and it frees them to make a positive difference in the world.

It is time for you to learn the skills and develop the awareness to become a positive change-maker. The more of us there are, the quicker it will occur.

This training is about learning to do just that!

Warriors of the Heart will serve you wherever you wish to increase communication and decrease anxiety and conflict

. . . with your family
. . . with your clients and customers
. . . with your students
. . . with your support group

and because you are intimately connected to everything, the reduction in conflict in your own life reduces the tension on our entire planet. This is the training that you take for all of us.

For a schedule of Danaan's workshops, write Earthstewards Network, Box 10697, Bainbridge Island, WA 98110.

Activities and Organizations
for
Warriors of the Heart

The groups listed here offer a wide variety of services to individuals and to our planet. Needless to say, there are hundreds more available, and we invite you to share them with us by sending a description and literature on them to the Earthstewards Network. We hope you will make some satisfying new connections in browsing through the list and we look forward to hearing from you.

Amnesty International USA
322 Eighth Avenue
New York NY 10001
(212)807-8400

An independent worldwide movement working impartially for the release of all prisoners of conscience, fair and prompt trials for political prisoners and an end to torture and executions.

Association for Research and Enlightenment, Inc.
PO Box 595
67th Street and Atlantic Ave.
Virginia Beach VA 23451
(804)428-3588

A living network of people who are finding a deeper meaning in life through the psychic work of Edgar Cayce. On the leading edge in such areas as holistic health care, meditation instruction, reincarnation studies and spiritual healing. Publications, field seminars, Study Groups and membership mailings.

Center for Citizen Initiatives
3268 Sacramento Street
San Francisco CA 94115
(415)346-1875

A non-profit, citizen-initiated organization dedicated to improving the quality of communication between the United States and the Soviet Union, to reducing US-USSR hostility by bringing Soviet and American peoples together in non-political, trust-building encounters and projects, and to providing updated, balanced public education on US-USSR issues to a broad spectrum of American citizens.

Chinook Learning Center
P.O. Box 57
Clinton WA 98236
(206)321-1884

A non-profit educational center and community dedicated to exploring a comprehensive vision of the future through programs focusing on personal, regional and global issues. Their perspective is spiritually-based, especially inspired by humanity's new relationship with the earth. Offers a variety of workshops, conferences and long-term programs to help people develop the understanding and the skills to effect positive change in themselves and in the world.

Connect/US-USSR
Suite 109, 430 Oak Grove St.
Minneapolis MN 55403
(612)871-5722

A non-profit organization working to foster educational and cultural exchanges between the United States and the Soviet Union. Includes professional exchanges, the hosting of Soviet visitors, and the facilitation of educational and cultural programs. The purpose of these connections is to educate Americans and Soviets about one another and to build mutually beneficial relationships between the people of the two countries.

Creative Response
9502 Lee Highway, Ste. B
Fairfax, VA 22031
(703) 385-4494

Producers of a peace play enacted by children of the world. The lively story deals with the nations in conflict and how children lead the world to peace.

Earthstewards Network
P.O. Box 10697
Bainbridge Island WA 98110
(206) 842-7986

Personal and global expansion of consciousness, spiritual awareness for creation of positive alternatives; workshops, publications, tapes, trips, posters, newsletter and journal.

The Fellowship of Reconciliation
P.O. Box 271
Nyack NY 10960
(914) 358-4601

A group of women and men who recognize the essential unity of all humanity and have joined together to explore the power of love and truth for resolving human conflict. Committed to the achievement of a just and peaceful world community, with full dignity and freedom for every human being. Seeks the company of people of faith who will respond to conflict nonviolently, seeking reconciliation through compassionate action.

Findhorn Community
Forres IV 36 OTZ
Scotland
(01309) 690582

Global consciousness, spiritual evolution, community; guest programs, books, tapes, One Earth journal.

Foundation for Global Community
222 High Street
Palo Alto CA 94301
(415) 328-7756

A nonprofit, non-partisan foundation whose goal is to educate through public presentations, writings, group discussion, and audio-visual techniques, that in the nuclear age, war is obsolete as a means of resolving conflict; and to research and develop educational processes through which an individual can discover and become personally involved, working in cooperation with people of all nations, races, and religions, to build a world beyond war.

Gesundheit Institute
1630 Robert Walker Place
Arlington VA 22207
(703) 525-8169

Building a 'no-charge' hospital with a humorous context.
Patch Adams, M.D.

Greenpeace
1436 U. St., N.W.
Washington DC 20009
(202)462-1177

Courageous ecological action to save endangered species,
especially whales and seals.

Institute of Cultural Affairs
4750 North Sheridan Road
Chicago IL 60640
(312)769-6363

A private, not-for-profit, research training and demonstration group concerned with the human factor in world development. Committed to serve in the process of improving the quality of human life through participatory problem- solving techniques, curriculum designs, educational methods and conferences. Focus is on helping people help themselves.

Institute for Soviet-American Relations
Suite 301, 1601 Connecticut Avenue, NW
Washington DC 20009
(202)387-3034

Makes connections between people, ideas and systems to help weave the fabric of Soviet-American relations. Publishes Surviving Together: A Journal of Soviet-American Relations, reflecting the good news about Soviet-American relations - exchanges, public education programs, current affairs in the USSR, official contacts, etc. Also publishes a Handbook of Organizations Involved in Soviet-American Relations.

Oxfam America
26 West Street
Boston MA 02111-1206
(617)482-1211

A non-profit, international agency that funds self-help development projects and disaster relief in poor countries in Africa, Asia, and Latin America, and also prepares and distributes educational materials for Americans on issues of development and hunger.

Peace Links
747 8th Street, SE
Washington DC 20003
(202)544-0805

A nationwide network of women who are reaching and activating an entirely new constituency of people who have made a commitment to preventing nuclear war. Includes personal and political action, educational materials and events.

Search for Common Ground
Suite 200, 1601 Connecticut Ave., NW
Washington DC 20009
(202) 265-4300

Effective organization for bringing together leaders of opposing factions and beliefs to discover "common ground."

Seva Foundation
8 N. St. Pedro Rd.
San Rafael CA 94903
(415) 492-1829

An international service organization of caring people dedicated to relieving suffering. Seva is the Sanskrit word for service. The Seva family comprises supporters from 36 countries with many different philosophical, religious and political views. All are bound together by a common vision of a world in which serving others is the most precious product of our lives.

Sierra Club
730 Polk St.
San Francisco CA 94109
(415) 776-2211

A non-profit, member-supported, organization that promotes conservation of the natural environment by influencing public policy decisions - legislative, administrative, legal, and electoral. Active with education and has many publications.

Sirius Community
Baker Road
Shutesbury MA 01072
(413) 259-1251

Spiritual community and educational center. Books, retreats, education, workshops, tapes, slide shows.

Worldwatch Institute
1776 Massachusetts Avenue, N.W.
Washington DC 20036
(202) 452-1999

An independent nonprofit research organization established to alert decision makers and the general public to emerging global trends in the availability and management of resources — both human and natural. Analyzes issues from a global perspective and within an interdisciplinary framework. Books and other publications available.

Earthstewards Network

Earthstewards have committed themselves to the spreading of consciousness, based upon the Sevenfold Path of Peace:

When we are at peace within our own hearts we shall be at peace with everyone and with our Mother the Earth.

When we recognize that our planet itself is a living organism co-evolving with humankind we shall become worthy of stewardship.

When we see ourselves as stewards of our planet and not as owners and masters of it there shall be lasting satisfaction from our labors.

When we accept the concept of Right Livelihood as the basic right of all we shall have respect for one another.

When we respect the sacredness of all life we shall be truly free.

When we free ourselves from our attachment to our ego-personalities we shall be able to experience our Oneness.

When we experience our Oneness — our total connected-ness with all beings — we shall be at peace within our own hearts.

As an Earthsteward, you will receive materials from many sources and be part of a network which will assist you in turning the thrust of humanity toward more holistic, loving, sharing relationships with each other and with all life forms, including our planet itself.

A commitment that you make as an Earthsteward is to develop a program of action which relates the concepts of the Sevenfold Path of Peace to your daily life. This commitment is to yourself and only you can define what it shall be. Material is provided to assist you in your planning, but you alone create the nature of the commitment. In this way, Earthstewards everywhere are literally changing the world. Our present world of aggression, excess, and isolation will not be changed by massive counter-movements; it will be transformed by you and me and thousands like us who make a commitment, who take on a sacred obligation to make a difference in whatever ways we can, with the tools we now have. Don't be worried about identifying what you can do. The function of the Earthstewards Network is to assist you in discovering your own path of service, and the network is a wonderful support group to call upon.

It is also suggested that you, as an Earthsteward, practice tithing to any groups, organizations, or projects that you consider worthy of your support. Tithing is an ancient, well-proven concept; the number ten (tithe) is significant. Many Earthstewards allocate 10% of some segment of their financial resources (10% of gross income or net income or "pocket" money, etc.) to worthwhile efforts. Casting your bread upon waters is a powerful way of linking your consciousness with that of all consciousness on our planet. It is important that you as an Earthsteward take responsibility for the expenditure of your money as well as your time and energy. No one will ask you about your tithing commitment; this is an agreement with yourself.

If you are ready to make a commitment, then you are ready to take your place in the Earthstewards Network. Please complete the application form so the network can send information and materials to help you in creating your plan of action. You and the world stand on the brink of the next level of consciousness. For your own transformation — for our planet's transformation — take the leap. Become an Earthsteward!

I don't know what your destiny will be,
but one thing I do know:
the only ones among you who will be really
happy are those who have sought and found
how to serve.

Albert Schweitzer

YOUR ARE INVITED
TO BECOME A PART OF
THE EARTHSTEWARDS NETWORK

Name _____

Telephone _____ Date _____

Street Address _____ City _____

State _____ Zip _____

May we print your name, address, and telephone number in our annual
Earthstewards Network Directory?   ☐ Yes   ☐ No

When you become an Earthsteward you will be a part of an exciting network
of people who support one another as they co-create a more peaceful,
caring world. You can choose to be part of:

- Our worldwide directory, a networking took where you can create your
  own message to let people know about you, about your dreams, about
  your business, whatever.
- Our travel host network which is comprised of Earthstewards around
  the world willing to serve as hosts to other Earthstewards traveling
  through their area. This is a great way to connect with others and save
  on travel expenses.
- Our Network Circles, where you can link-up with new friends with
  common interests, common concerns and shared values.
- Our Warriors of the Heart and Essential Peacemaking/Women and Men
  trainings, where we learn valuable tools for resolving our conflicts and
  dealing with gender issues.
- Our grassroots diplomacy adventures, where we have gone to the
  Middle East, Russian, N. Ireland, Central America, India, Nepal, China,
  etc., where we can learn what it's really like to be a part of a global family.
- Our Peace Trees projects, where we bring together young adults from
  around the world to plant trees, restore the environment, and learn the
  communication and conflict resolution skills needed to create lasting
  trust.

In addition you will receive our quarterly network newsletter, your intimate
connection to this new family of positive change-makers around the world,
and regular informational updates concerning projects and programs.

☐ I am enclosing a check for $25 (U.S. $35 for foreign membership) and wish
to be included in the Earthstewards Network. Make checks payable to the
Earthstewards Network.

Earthstewards Network, PO Box 10697, Bainbridge Island, WA 98110
206-842-7986

Sunstone Publications

We hope you have enjoyed **Warriors of the Heart** as we are glad to have been able to share it with you. If you would like another copy for a friend or would like to purchase one of our other books, they are described below.

Warriors of the Heart is a handbook for bringing harmony to all our relationships, personal and planetary, based on conflict-resolution workshops and techniques used by the author throughout the world. 224 pp. Danaan Parry.($9.95)

The Earthsteward's Handbook is a collection of reflections and practical suggestions on ways to help make the spiritual vision of peace a reality in our life together on this planet. This is an updated and larger book version of the older handbook. 160 pp. Danaan Parry and Lila Forest ($6.95)

The Essene Book of Days is a journal, calendar and guide for those on a path of personal and spiritual growth. Each daily page has an opening ritual, meditation, blessing, focus for the day, moon phase and sign, sun's light and sign and a place to record feelings. Also contains several teaching stories, information about the Essenes and the holidays surrounding the solstices, equinoxes, and cross-quarter days. 416 pp. Danaan Parry($14.95)

Essene Engagement Book is a spiral-bound daily appointment book which fits easily in a purse, portfolio or backpack. Each two - page spread shows every day of the week with moon phases, sun signs, holidays and room for notes. ($9.95)

Essene Book of Meditations and Blessings is a handy pocket-size book featuring all the daily meditations and blessings in *The Essene Book of Days*. A great travel companion! 128 pp. Danaan Parry ($4.95)

Astro-Dome® 3D Map of the Night Sky contains everything you need to construct a 20" planetarium. Stars glow in the dark and a 24-page Constellation Handbook is included. Klaus Hunig ($9.95)

Astro-Dots is a unique coloring book in which children connect dots and stars to create the constellations. Fun and educational! ($3.95)

To order: Include $3.50 for shipping and handling for the first item, and $1.50 for each additional item. Send check, money order or VISA/MasterCard number to: Sunstone Publications, P.O. Box 788AW, Cooperstown, NY 13326. Or phone (800) 327-0306. NY residents please add appropriate sales tax. *Call or write for our free catalog!*